THE ABUNDANT LIFE
BIBLE
AMPLIFIER

DANIEL
1-7

WILLIAM H. SHEA

THE ABUNDANT LIFE
BIBLE
AMPLIFIER

DANIEL
1-7

Prophecy As History

GEORGE R. KNIGHT
General Editor

Pacific Press Publishing Association
Boise, Idaho
Oshawa, Ontario, Canada

Edited by B. Russell Holt
Designed by Tim Larson
Typeset in 11/14 Janson Text

Copyright © 1996 by
Pacific Press Publishing Association
Printed in the United States of America
All Rights Reserved

Maps on pages 53, 141, 147, 153, and 159 taken from Zondervan
NIV Atlas of the Bible by Carl Rasmussen. Copyright © 1989 by
Carta, Jerusalem. Used by permission of Zondervan Publishing
House.

Unless otherwise mentioned, all Bible quotations in this book are
from the New International Version, and all emphasis in Bible quotations is supplied by the author.

ISBN 0-8163-1340-7 (paper)
ISBN 0-8163-1341-5 (hard)

96 97 98 99 00 • 5 4 3 2 1

CONTENTS

List of Maps 6
General Preface 9
Author's Preface 11
How to Use This Book 15
Introduction to the Book of Daniel 19
List of Works Cited 27

Volume One: Prophecy As History
    1. Interpreting History 33
    2. Exiled (1) 49
    3. Fallen Kings (4, 5) 69
    4. Kingly Persecution (3, 6) 101
    5. Fallen Kingdoms (2, 7) 131

MAPS

Map of the Ancient Near East   53
Map of Babylon and Its Environs   79
Map of the Neo-Babylonian Empire   141
Map of the Persian Empire   147
Map of the Empire of Alexander the Great (Greek Empire)   153
Map of the Roman Empire   159
Map of the Greek Empire Divided   165
Map of the Roman Empire divided   171

DEDICATION

To Karen

GENERAL PREFACE

The Abundant Life Bible Amplifier series is aimed at helping readers understand the Bible better. Rather than merely offering comments on or about the Bible, each volume seeks to enable people to study their Bibles with fuller understanding.

To accomplish that task, scholars who are also proven communicators have been selected to author each volume. The basic idea underlying this combination is that scholarship and the ability to communicate on a popular level are compatible skills.

While the Bible Amplifier is written with the needs and abilities of laypeople in mind, it will also prove helpful to pastors and teachers. Beyond individual readers, the series will be useful in church study groups and as guides to enrich participation in the weekly prayer meeting.

Rather than focusing on the details of each verse, the Bible Amplifier series seeks to give readers an understanding of the themes and patterns of each biblical book as a whole and how each passage fits into that context. As a result, the series does not seek to solve all the problems or answer all the questions that may be related to a given text. In the process of accomplishing the goal for the series, both inductive and explanatory methodologies are used.

Each volume in this series presents its author's understanding of the biblical book being studied. As such, it does not necessarily represent the "official" position of the Seventh-day Adventist Church.

It should be noted that the Bible Amplifier series utilizes the New International Version of the Bible as its basic text. *Every reader should read the "How to Use This Book" section to get the fullest benefit from the Bible Amplifier study volumes.*

Dr. William H. Shea is an associate director of the Biblical Research Institute in Silver Spring, Maryland. Before coming to his present position, Dr. Shea served as a professor of Old Testament at the Seventh-day Adventist Theological Seminary at Andrews University. He holds doctoral degrees in both medicine and Near Eastern studies. A prolific author, Dr. Shea has written scores of articles and reviews for both scholarly and popular journals. He has taken a special interest in the book of Daniel. Many readers of this volume will be familiar with his *Selected Studies on Prophetic Interpretation*.

George R. Knight
Berrien Springs, Michigan

AUTHOR'S PREFACE

An exciting archaeological rediscovery has interest for students of Daniel's life and writings. Near Jerusalem, a number of what were probably royal tombs were excavated in the 1920s by Raymond Weill, but slipped from the attention of the archaeological community. Interest in these tombs was revived by an article in the January/February 1995 issue of *Biblical Archaeology Review* titled, "Is This David's Tomb?" The article discussed the possibility that the largest of these tombs, one located on the south side of the cemetery, is King David's burial site.

Not noted in the article, however, is that on the *north* side of the cemetery is a short stairway of about a dozen steps with a tomb at the top and one at the bottom. The tomb at the bottom of the stairway is actually cut into the middle of the bottom step. This tomb is of special interest in terms of this book, because writing on the tomb itself indicates that the prophet Daniel was buried here! Just above the tomb's entry is inscribed the Hebrew word, *qeber*, "tomb." To the left is the Hebrew word for "this," so that the phrase thus far means, "This is the tomb of . . . ." One expects a personal name to appear next, and this is the case. On the left lower side of the step's front face, written in a pre-exilic type of Hebrew, is the name *d'any'el*, "Daniel," with the Hebrew vowel letters actually written into the word! The final word of the inscription, in the lower left corner below the name, is the title, *nabi'*, or "prophet." Thus the entire sentence reads, "This is the tomb of the prophet Daniel."

Another extremely interesting feature of this tomb is the artwork carved in relief on the right side of the entryway. There is a scene of a man being thrown down, or falling—suggesting Daniel being cast into a lions' den. Above this is a picture of a man climbing out of a round hole, depicting Daniel's escape from the den of lions. Along the bottom right side are two lions, a large one in the middle and a smaller one in the far right corner of the step. The large one is facing away from the figure of Daniel, the smaller one is facing toward him, but neither seems to be interested in doing him any harm. The scenes illustrating this great event of deliverance in Daniel's life are especially fitting for his tomb. Just as he emerged from the lions' den unharmed because of his faith in the God he served, so Daniel will one day come forth in the resurrection from his burial place—also because of his faith in the Saviour.

The location of Daniel's tomb has been uncertain until this discovery. In Susa, the biblical Shushan, a tomb has been traditionally designated as that of the prophet, but solid support for that tradition has been lacking. Now, with this new evidence from Jerusalem, it seems clear that the tradition of the tomb in Susa is incorrect.

Whether Daniel traveled to Jerusalem prior to his death or whether his body was taken there for burial after he died in Babylon, we do not know. We do know that he was still alive in Babylon as late as the third year of Cyrus (see Daniel 10:1). The tomb in Jerusalem was cut in the early Persian period, according to contextual indications, so the assumption is that Daniel was buried there soon after he died—whether his death occurred in Babylon or Jerusalem. The tomb has not been explored inside recently, but the bones are most probably not present, as is the case with most of the tombs in this cemetery.

In this first volume of the two-volume study on Daniel in the Bible Amplifier series, we will be looking at the historical chapters of Daniel's book. These encompass, for the most part, the biblical details of the life of this remarkable man of God. (Volume Two will deal with the prophetic portions of Daniel.)

The history brought to view in Daniel is a special kind of history—a theological history in which selected events are given, while others are ignored. Of course, his own personal participation was one major factor in Daniel's selection of which events to record. There is something autobiographical about the historical chapters of Daniel's book. But they are more than just the story of what happened to Daniel in Babylon. They also reveal the hand of God in history and in Daniel's life. Thus, we can study Daniel 6 to see if there really was a historical figure such as Darius the Mede. But more importantly, we can also see how God acted on Daniel's behalf at this time in Babylon's history. Above and behind the historical accounts given in Daniel is the overarching perspective of the interaction of God in human history to work out His own eternal purposes.

In this way, history and theology come together. In Daniel, we have a selective religious history that reveals not only the political history of nations at that time, but also God's interaction with them and with His people who lived in these nations.

Beyond that, the history of the book gives us the context and starting point for the prophecies that we will be studying in the second volume in this series. In Daniel, history and prophecy are not to be set apart in separate realms; they are interwoven. The two blend as the prophecies begin in the historical time of the prophet himself and then extend into the future beyond the prophet's day. Daniel actually lived under the first two of the nations found in the "outline" prophecies of the book—Babylon, Medo-Persia, Greece, and Rome. And the fulfillment of those prophecies beyond his time have given testimony to the inspired nature of the prophecies given to him.

The final reason we need to carefully study the historical chapters of Daniel is for the spiritual lessons we can learn from them. In the reaction of Daniel and his friends to the pagan culture of Babylon, we can find an example of how to live in the pagan culture of our own century. Their lives can provide a model for the way we should live today—honest, dedicated to God, and courageous in His faith.

William H. Shea
Silver Spring, Maryland

How to Use This Book

The Abundant Life Amplifier series treats each major portion of each Bible book in five main sections.

The first section is called "Getting Into the Word." The purpose of this section is to encourage readers to study their own Bibles. For that reason, the text of the Bible has not been printed in the volumes in this series.

You will get the most out of your study if you work through the exercises in each of the "Getting Into the Word" sections. This will not only aid you in learning more about the Bible but will also increase your skill in using Bible tools and in asking (and answering) meaningful questions about the Bible.

It will be helpful if you write out the answers and keep them in a notebook or file folder for each biblical book. Writing out your thoughts will enhance your understanding. The benefit derived from such study, of course, will be proportionate to the amount of effort expended.

The "Getting Into the Word" sections assume that the reader has certain minimal tools available. Among these are a concordance and a Bible with maps and marginal cross-references. If you don't have a New International Version of the Bible, we recommend that you obtain one for use with this series, since all the Bible Amplifier authors are using the NIV as their basic text. For the same reason, your best choice of a concordance is the *NIV Exhaustive Concordance*, edited by E. W. Goodrick and J. R. Kohlenberger. Strong's *Exhaustive Concordance of the Bible* and Young's *Analytical Concordance to the Bible* are also useful. However, even if all you have is Cruden's *Concordance*, you will be able to do all of the "Getting Into the Word" exercises and most of the "Researching the Word" exercises.

The "Getting Into the Word" sections also assume that the reader has a Bible dictionary. The *Seventh-day Adventist Bible Dictionary* is quite helpful, but those interested in greater depth may want to acquire the four-volume *International Standard Bible Encyclopedia* (1974-1988 edition) or the six-volume *Anchor Bible Dictionary*.

The second section in the treatment of the biblical passages is called "Exploring the Word." The purpose of this section is to discuss the major themes in each biblical book. Thus the comments will typically deal with fairly large portions of Scripture (often an entire chapter) rather than providing a verse-by-verse treatment, such as is found in the *Seventh-day Adventist Bible Commentary*. In fact, many verses and perhaps whole passages in some biblical books may be treated minimally or passed over altogether.

Another thing that should be noted is that the purpose of the "Exploring the Word" sections is not to respond to all the problems or answer all the questions that might arise in each passage. Rather, as stated above, the "Exploring the Word" sections are to develop the Bible writers' major themes. In the process, the author of each volume will bring the best of modern scholarship into the discussion and thus enrich the reader's understanding of the biblical passage at hand. The "Exploring the Word" sections will also develop and provide insight into many of the issues first raised in the "Getting Into the Word" exercises.

The third section in the treatment of the biblical passage is "Applying the Word." This section is aimed at bringing the lessons of each passage into daily life. Once again, you may want to write out a response to these questions and keep them in your notebook or file folder on the biblical book being studied.

The fourth section, "Researching the Word," is for those students who want to delve more deeply into the Bible passage under study or into the history behind it. It is recognized that not everyone will have the research tools for this section. Those expecting to use the research sections should have an exhaustive Bible concordance, the *Seventh-day Adventist Bible Commentary*, a good Bible dictionary, and a Bible atlas. It will also be helpful to have several versions of the Bible.

The final component in each chapter of this book will be a list of recommendations for "Further Study of the Word." While most readers will not have all of these works, many of them may be available in local libraries. Others can be purchased through your local book dealer. It is assumed that many users of this series will already own the seven-volume *Seventh-day Adventist Bible Commentary* and the one-volume *Seventh-day Adventist Bible Dictionary*.

In closing, it should be noted that while a reader will learn much about the Bible from a *reading* of the books in the Bible Amplifier series, he or she will gain infinitely more by *studying* the Bible in connection with that reading.

The Book of Daniel

One of the best ways to study a book of the Bible is to read it thoughtfully and prayerfully from beginning to end in as short a time as possible. The following suggestions will help you to get the most out of a thoughtful reading of Daniel.

1. **As you read Daniel, list on a page in your Daniel notebook what you consider to be the main point or idea for each chapter. How does that point or idea contribute to the book's developing theme?**
2. **For each chapter, list or underline at least one idea or text that is of special importance to your spiritual journey. Why is that thought so special or precious to you?**

Daniel and His Book

This survey of the book begins with a brief review of the author's personal biography. We should become acquainted with Daniel the man before we come to the subject of Daniel the prophet.

Daniel was born in the late seventh century B.C. and lived his early years in Jerusalem or its vicinity. By the time he had grown to manhood, political and military struggles in the great nations of his time altered the fate of little Judah in which he lived. From the time of Daniel's birth until 605 B.C., Judah was nominally under the control of Egypt. In that year, however, a major battle took place; Egypt was defeated, and Babylon came to exercise control over Judah and Jerusalem. Nebuchadnezzar II, commander of the Babylonian army, led his troops to the gates of Jerusalem and demanded the payment of tribute and a selection of choice hostages. Daniel was among those chosen. He was selected, along with the others, because of his future potential as a civil servant in Babylon—a task he fulfilled, after the requisite training period, for more than sixty years.

But God had something more in mind for Daniel than mere service at the court of Babylon. God called him to the office of prophet and gave him dreams and visions. Some of these dreams, visions, and prophetic statements were addressed to the people of his time. On three different occasions, Daniel was given prophecies which dealt with, or were delivered to, kings at the royal court in Babylon. This type of prophecy—dealing with contemporary persons and issues—is sometimes called *classical* prophecy. Daniel spoke with prophetic voice to the kings of Babylon just as Jeremiah spoke to the kings in Jerusalem.

On other occasions, he was given prophecies which involved a longer range of vision, looking into the future history of the nations. This second type of prophecy is commonly called *apocalyptic* prophecy because it deals more specifically with revealing the future. It is also called outline prophecy because it outlines the history of nations in advance.

Thus in Daniel's book we find these two different types of prophecies—classical and apocalyptic. We also find another distinct type of narrative—history. Different sections of the book clearly contain these different types of literature. In general, the book of Daniel divides in half; the first half is history, and the second half is prophecy. It is in the first half of the book—in the context of history—that we find the classical prophecies that deal with contemporary persons and events. The prophecies of the second half of the book are more apocalyptic in character.

The languages used in Daniel's book also emphasize the distinction between the two main sections. Most of the historical chapters were written in Aramaic, while most of the prophetic chapters were written in Hebrew. Hebrew was Daniel's native tongue, and Aramaic was a related language that was used for part of the official correspondence of the Neo-Babylonian and Persian Empires. More than any other book in the Bible, Daniel is bilingual. Ezra was also written in both Hebrew and Aramaic, but only a small part of Ezra—the royal decrees—is in Aramaic.

This twofold nature of Daniel provides a convenient outline with which to study the book. In this Bible Amplifier series, the study of Daniel will be presented in two volumes. Volume 1 will deal with the historical chapters, and volume 2 will focus on the prophetic chapters. Because of the different types of material in Daniel, both the historical and prophetic volumes will contain their own introductory chapters dealing in detail with historical and prophetic issues respectively. The introduction to the historical chapters will take up some issues regarding the date of the composition of the book. Some commentaries on Daniel hold that this book was not written by a single individual, Daniel, who lived in sixth-century B.C. Babylon, but rather by an unknown, anonymous author who lived in Judea in the second century B.C. The nature of the materials found in the historical chapters bear upon this question which is explored in the introduction to the historical section.

The prophecies of Daniel also have been interpreted in very different ways. Three main schools of thought exist on the interpretation of Daniel's prophecies. *(1) Preterist.* This method of interpretation places all the emphasis on the past and sees the fulfillment of portions of the prophecies as past. *(2) Futurist.* This school of thought places the fulfillment of portions of Daniel in the future. *(3) Historicist.* This view of the prophecies emphasizes a flow and continuity from the past through the present and into the as-yet-unfulfilled future. It is sometimes called the continuous historical view, because it sees the prophecies as part of a continuum from the past to the future. The introduction to the prophetic section of Daniel's book explores the strengths and weaknesses of each of these schools of interpretation. The approach taken in the two volumes in this Bible Amplifier series falls in the category of the historicist view.

Daniel's experience included more than just being a historical figure. There was even more to Daniel than his experience as a prophet.

There was also the matter of his own personal spiritual experience with God. This side of his experience and his book should not be neglected or overwhelmed by the other elements. The last chapter of volume 2 considers the important matter of Daniel's own spiritual experience as a chosen instrument of God.

So that will be the order of march in the two volumes covering Daniel: history, prophecy, and spiritual experience.

A Note on the Order of Treatment

The reader will notice that the order in which these volumes on Daniel take up the different aspects of his book varies somewhat from the standard and canonical order of the chapters in the book itself. However, if one looks carefully at the datelines of the biblical chapters—when they are given—it is apparent that Daniel does not present his material in strict chronological order either. For example, the prophecies of Daniel, chapters 7 and 8, were actually given *before* the historical events of chapters 5 and 6. Although all of the events recorded in Daniel are historical in the sense that they actually happened, they have been arranged in a certain way for a certain purpose. *To a degree, this study on Daniel has endeavored to follow the thought order rather than the written order. For that reason, the reader will find some irregularity in the order in which the chapters are presented.*

In volume 1, the historical section, the chapters studied follow something of an inverted order. Chapters 2 and 7 have been grouped together because they are concerned with prophecies about the nations. Chapters 3 and 6 have been grouped together because they deal with persecution of the Jews in exile, Daniel and his three friends in particular. Chapters 4 and 5 have been grouped together because they deal with Nebuchadnezzar and Belshazzar, the kings of Babylon. This type of inverted order is sometimes known as a *chiasm* (from the Greek letter *chi* which looks like an X). That something like this was intended by the original author is evident from the fact that it is precisely these six historical chapters that were written in the Aramaic language.

When we come to the prophetic chapters, the order is not inverted; rather, it is reversed. Thus we have chosen to study the three main prophetic chapters in the heart of the book of Daniel in reverse order; beginning with chapter 9, then going on to chapter 8, followed by chapter 7, and finally concluding that section with a summary of these three chapters. The reason for this order of study has to do with thought order, not chronological or historical order. In terms of the events to which these prophecies refer, chapter 9 comes first because it focuses especially upon the Messiah. The contents of chapter 8 go on well beyond that point into the Christian Era. But it is Daniel 7 which carries the prophecy on into the final kingdom of God and pictures the saints of the Most High as entering and possessing it.

There is a reason for following this thought order; it is not the arbitrary selection of a modern commentator who simply wants to do something different. In modern western-European thought, we reason from cause to effect. We collect all the data and then synthesize it into a hypothesis. Finally, we refine that hypothesis to a theory. That is the procedure of the modern scientific method.

But the ancients were not moderns nor were they scientists, so they worked out things in their own way. While they were quite capable of working through things in chronological order as we do, they also utilized an approach that involved reasoning from effect back to cause. The prophets could depict a scene in such a way that their listeners were led to inquire, "Why did this happen?" This question led them back to the cause. An inspired prophet could say, "This land will be destroyed and left desolate," leading back to the natural question, "Why will this land be destroyed?" The answer to that question commonly lay in the fact that the people to whom the prophet was sent were a wicked and rebellious people who had broken their covenant with God. For an example of this approach, see Jeremiah, chapters 4 through 7, and Micah, chapter 1. Wickedness was the cause, and desolation was the result— but the prophet gave the result first in order to lead his readers to a discussion of the cause.

That is the kind of thought order followed in these three prophecies at the heart of Daniel. If Daniel were presenting these prophecies to a modern audience today, he would naturally give chapter 9 first, because that chapter deals with the first events to happen. He would follow with chapter 8 because that prophecy presents the next events to happen. Finally, he would give chapter 7 because that prophecy presents the grand climax to the series. Only when these prophecies are put in this thought order does the modern reader appreciate fully their great sweep and connection with each other— something that would have come more naturally to an ancient listener or reader because of the way in which his or her thought processes had been conditioned. By reversing Daniel's original order of presentation, we have attempted to unveil the full beauty of the way in which these prophecies were first presented.

The final major line of prophecy in Daniel's book is found in chapters 10–12. Chapter 10 presents the introduction, or prologue, to this prophecy, and chapter 12 contains its epilogue, or conclusion. The body of the prophecy in chapter 11 is very detailed and follows a historical and chronological order.

There are four major apocalyptic, or outline, prophecies in the book of Daniel. They are found in chapters 2, 7, 8, and 11. Outline prophecies cover the rise and fall of nations from the prophet's day to the end of time.

The other major prophecy in Daniel's book is found at the end of chapter 9. While the four major outline prophecies deal with the rise and fall of nations, chapter 9 deals more exclusively with the people of Daniel's city and country—Jerusalem and Judah. Although the events of this prophecy run parallel to those of the other major outline prophecies, they focus upon a particular part of that world not covered in the other prophecies—the history of the Jewish people in Judea down to the time of the Messiah. The fact that the four major lines of prophecy in this book go over the same outline of nations is called *recapitulation*, or *parallelism*. Just as the four Gospels go over the same events from different perspectives, so these four lines of complementary prophecies go over the same territory, filling in more details each time. The presentation starts out on the broadest scale in chapter 2, with the nations represented by different metals in an image. By the time we reach chapter 11, we are down to the individual kings of each nation and their personal actions. Chapter 2 starts out with the use of the telescope, while chapter 11 ends up with the use of the microscope.

The final chapter of volume 2 on Daniel in the Bible Amplifier series ends on the theme of spiritual relationship. This element is found not so much in the prophecy itself as in the experience of the prophet. That is where I feel it should also end up for the reader of this book.

Outline of the Book of Daniel

A standard outline of the contents of the book of Daniel is organized something like this:

    I.   Daniel's exile (1:1-21)
   II.   Nebuchadnezzar's dream: an outline prophecy (2:1-49)
  III.   The great image: Daniel's friends vindicated (3:1-30)
  IV.   The king is mad: Nebuchadnezzar's illness (4:1-37)
   V.   The night that Babylon fell: Belshazzar's end (5:1-31)
  VI.   Daniel in and out of the lions' den (6:1-28)
 VII.   Daniel's dream: an outline prophecy (7:1-28)
VIII.   Daniel's vision: an outline prophecy (8:1-27)
  IX.   The seventy weeks: Gabriel's prophecy about the Jews (9:1-27)
   X.   The appearance of God to Daniel (10:1-21)
  XI.   Gabriel's prophecy: an outline prophecy (11:1-45)
 XII.   Epilogue: dates for the previous prophecy (12:1-13)

Because we have chosen to follow a more literary and thematic order in this study of Daniel, these chapters have been rearranged to the following order:

    I.   Exiled (1:1-21)
   II.   Fallen kings (4:1–5:31)
  III.   Persecution (3:1-30; 6:1-28)
  IV.   Fallen kingdoms (2:1-49; 7:1-28)
   V.   Christ as sacrifice (9:1-27)
  VI.   Christ as priest (8:1-27)
 VII.   Christ as king (7:1-28)
VIII.   The final message (10:1–12:13)

For Further Reading

1. For a general survey of how Daniel has been interpreted through the years, see the article, "History of the Interpretation of Daniel," in F. D. Nichol, ed., *The Seventh-day Adventist Bible Commentary*, 4:39-78.
2. For a more contemporary and popularized exposition of Daniel's prophecies, see C. Mervyn Maxwell, *God Cares*, vol. 1.
3. For a more dated, but detailed, treatment of the entire book of Daniel, see Uriah Smith, *Thoughts on Daniel*.

LIST OF WORKS CITED

Blenkinsopp, Joseph. *A History of Prophecy in Israel.* Philadelphia: Westminster, 1983.

Chiera, Edward. *They Wrote on Clay.* Phoenix paperback ed. Chicago: University of Chicago, 1956.

Comba, Emilio. *History of the Waldenses in Italy.* London: Truslove and Shirley, 1889.

de Liguori, Alphonses. *Dignity and Duties of the Priest; or, Selva.* Brooklyn, N.Y.: Redemptionist Fathers, 1927.

Froom, Leroy Edwin. *The Prophetic Faith of Our Fathers.* 4 vols. Hagerstown, Md.: Review and Herald, 1946-1954.

Geiermann, Peter. *Convert's Catechism of Catholic Doctrine.* St. Louis: Herder, 1957.

Hasel, Gerhard F. "Interpretations of the Chronology of the Seventy Weeks." In *The Seventy Weeks, Leviticus, and the Nature of Prophecy.* Edited by Frank Holbrook, Daniel and Revelation Committee Series, vol. 3. Silver Spring, Md.: General Conference of Seventh-day Adventists, 1986.

Herodotus. *The Histories.* Loeb Classical Library. 4 vols. Translated by A. D. Godley. Cambridge: Harvard University, 1920-1925.

Heschel, Abraham J. *The Prophets.* 2 vols. New York: Harper, 1962.

Holbrook, Frank, ed. *Symposium on Daniel.* Daniel and Revelation Committee Series, vol. 2. Silver Spring, Md.: General Conference of Seventh-day Adventists, Biblical Research Institute, 1986.

Holbrook, Frank, ed. *The Seventy Weeks, Leviticus, and the Nature of Prophecy.* Daniel and Revelation Committee Series, vol. 3. Silver Spring, Md.: Bibilical Research Institute, General Conference of Seventh-day Adventists, 1986.

Horn, Siegfried H. *The Spade Confirms the Book.* Hagerstown, Md.: Review and Herald, 1957.

———. "New Light on Nebuchadnezzar's Madness." In *Ministry,* April

1978, 38-40.

———., et al. *Seventh-day Adventist Bible Dictionary*, rev. ed., Edited by Raymond H. Woolsey. Hagerstown, Md.: Review and Herald, 1979.

Horn, Siegfried H., and Lynn H. Wood. *The Chronology of Ezra* 7. Hagerstown, Md.: Review and Herald, 1953.

James, Edward. *The Franks*. Oxford: Basil-Blackwell, 1988.

Jerome's Commentary on Daniel. Translated by Gleason L. Archer. Grand Rapids, Mich.: Baker, 1958.

Kelly, V. J. *Forbidden Sunday and Feast-Day Occupations*. Washington, D.C.: Catholic University of America, 1943.

Kenyon, Kathleen. *Royal Cities of the Old Testament. London: Barrie and Jenkins, 1971.*

Kingdom, Robert M. *Myths About the St. Bartholomew's Day Massacres, 1572-1576*. Cambridge: Harvard University, 1988.

Ladurie, Emmanuel LeRoy. *Montaillou: The Promised Land of Terror.* Translated by Barbara Bray. New York: Vintage, 1979.

Lecky, W. E. H. *History of the Rise and Influence of the Spirit of Rationalism in Europe*. Reprint ed. New York: G. Braziller, 1955.

McHugh, J. A., and C. J. Callan. *Catechism of the Council of Trent for Parish Priests*. New York: Wagner, 1958.

Maxwell, C. Mervyn. *God Cares*, vol. 1. Boise, Idaho: Pacific Press, 1981.

Mayer, Hans E. *The Crusades*. 2nd ed. Oxford: Oxford University, 1988.

Neugebauer, Otto. *The Exact Sciences in Antiquity*. Paperback ed. New York: Dover, 1969.

Nichol, Francis D., ed. *Seventh-day Adventist Bible Commentary*. Rev. ed., 7 vols. Hagerstown, Md.: Review and Herald, 1976-1980.

O'Brien, John A. *The Faith of Millions: The Credentials of the Catholic Religion*. Huntington, Ind.: Our Sunday Visitor, 1963.

Polybius. *The Histories*. Loeb Classical Library. Cambridge: Harvard University.

Roux, Georges. *Ancient Iraq*. 3rd ed. New York: Viking Penguin, 1993.

Saggs, H. W. F. *The Greatness That Was Babylon*. New York: Hawthorn, 1962.

Seilhammer, F. H. *Prophets and Prophecy.* Philadelphia: Fortress, 1977.

Shea, William H. *Selected Studies in Prophetic Interpretation.* 2nd ed. Daniel and Revelation Committee Series, vol. 1. Silver Spring, Md.: Biblical Research Institute, General Conference of Seventh-day Adventists, 1992.

——. "Daniel 3: Extra-Biblical Texts and the Convocation on the Plain of Dura." *Andrews University Seminary Studies,* Vol. 20 (1982). 1:29-52.

——. "Darius the Mede: An Update." *Andrews University Seminary Studies.* Vol. 20 (1982) 3:229-248.

——. "Darius the Mede in His Persian-Babylonian Setting." *Andrews University Seminary Studies,* Vol. 29 (1991). 3:235-257.

Smith, Uriah. *Thoughts on Daniel.* Nashville: Southern Publishing Association, 1944.

Strand, Kenneth. *Interpreting the Book of Revelation.* 2nd ed. Naples, Fl.: Ann Arbor Publishers, 1979.

Wiseman, Donald J. *Chronicles of Chaldean Kings.* London: British Museum, 1956.

——., et al. *Notes on Some Problems in the Book of Daniel.* London: Tyndale, 1965.

Whitcomb, John C. *Darius the Mede.* Grand Rapids, Mich.: Eerdmans, 1959.

White, Ellen G. *The Great Controversy.* Boise, Idaho: Pacific Press, 1950.

——. *Patriarchs and Prophets.* Boise, Idaho: Pacific Press, 1958.

——. *Prophets and Kings.* Boise, Idaho: Pacific Press, 1943.

Xenophon. *Cyropaedia.* Loeb Classical Library. 2 vols. Translated by Walter Miller. Cambridge: Harvard University, 1914.

VOLUME ONE

Chapters 1–7

Prophecy As History

CHAPTER ONE

Interpreting History

The first half of Daniel, chapters 1 to 6, is essentially historical in nature. These historical narratives include some prophecy, but clearly they contain more history than prophecy. The historical nature of this portion of the book raises several significant questions:

- What is the biblical view of history?
- What is Daniel's view of history?
- Does the book address Neo-Babylonian history or some later period?
- What is God's activity in history? What is His relationship to it?

These questions all boil down to two main ones:

1. Does God interact with human history, or has He gone off to some other portion of His universe, leaving Earth to go along on its own?

2. With what period of history does Daniel's book deal?

The second question involves historicity more than history, and the text of the book itself gives a direct and readily available answer: Daniel's book presents itself as a record of the experiences of some persons who lived during the period of the Neo-Babylonian kingdom, during the late seventh and much of the sixth century B.C. But beyond this simple answer lies another issue: Is the book of Daniel

33

really a true record of events that happened in the sixth century B.C.? Or is it something that was written down later by someone other than the prophet Daniel to make it sound as if it occurred in the sixth century B.C.?

Many current commentaries on Daniel often answer these questions by taking the position that God does *not* intervene in human affairs and that the book was actually written in the second century B.C., not the sixth, by someone other than Daniel. Therefore, these commentators don't expect the book of Daniel to be historically accurate or true to the sixth century B.C. setting it describes. In down-to-earth language, this is what is known as "Daniel in the critics' den."

The Biblical View of History

Does God interact with human history? This is a philosophical question. It involves the biblical view of history and goes back to the question of the essential nature of Scripture at its very core. What is the Bible? More specifically to our discussion of Daniel's book, what is the Old Testament? It is a revelation of the nature, character, and purposes of God. But it is more than that. It provides a history that begins with Creation in Genesis and ends with Ezra and Nehemiah in the Persian period. That history extends through the books of Moses and Joshua, the book of Judges, 1 and 2 Samuel, and the books of Kings, paralleled by Chronicles. Finally, that history comes to an end with the records of Ezra and Nehemiah. In all, it extends over more than two millennia. But there is more to this history than mere raw records of what happened. There is a particular view of history, and that view is intimately involved with God as the central actor on the stage of that history. It is, as one historian-theologian has described it, a record of "the mighty acts of God." God has been active throughout all of that history, interacting with human beings, guiding and directing them, not only in terms of their earthly affairs, but also in terms of how to obtain His salvation.

This same view of history is also evident in the book of Daniel. Here, the story starts with the first conquest of Jerusalem, by

Nebuchadnezzar. This turn of events must have looked disastrous to many of the Jews living in Jerusalem at that time. Yet behind it all, God was working out His purposes. He permitted the conquest of Judah and Jerusalem because the nation was led by Jehoiakim, a wicked and rebellious king, and because its society was morally corrupt. Even in the tragedy of conquest, however, God brought good out of evil. His servants—Daniel and his friends—were brought into circumstances where they were able to witness in a way that extended far beyond their little family circle in Judah. They became witnesses for the true God among all the courtiers of Babylon and before the most powerful monarch of the time. God gave Jehoiakim into Nebuchadnezzar's hand, but He also gave favor to Daniel and his friends before that very same king. Thus, in the personal and national events of the time, we can see God's hand at work. And since we have the inspired word of the prophet Daniel who viewed those workings and was given information from heaven about them, we can see the intervention of God in these human circumstances all the more clearly.

We see God's intervention in human history in other aspects of Daniel as well. God not only intervenes in the course of history between nations, such as Babylon and Judah, but He also involves Himself in the history, the personal story, of individuals. For Daniel's friends, we see God's miraculous intervention, especially in chapter 3, with the story of their deliverance from the fiery furnace. In the case of Daniel, God's involvement is operative all the way through the book, but it comes especially to the forefront in chapter 6 with the miraculous deliverance of Daniel from the hungry lions in their lair. So God operates on the level of nations and historical events of epic proportions, but He also interacts with people on an individual level.

The third way in which the book of Daniel demonstrates God's attention to, and involvement in, the history of nations and individuals is through the prophecies given there. The four major outline prophecies of the book, those in chapters 2, 7, 8, and 11, provide a preview from the time of the prophet down through the ages of history to follow. God not only has an interest in the course of the history of the nations; He not only intervenes on occasion to affect it; but He also knows the course that it will take. Readers of the book of Daniel may rest assured that there is indeed a caring God behind the scenes of action in history.

This view of the world that is presented in Daniel and throughout the Bible is not very compatible with modern philosophical thought. The modern worldview has its origin not so much in the Bible as in the philosophy of the ancient Greeks. In particular, this modern worldview was shaped by revolutions in thought that occurred in the eighteenth century A.D., known as the Age of Reason. Working from the physical model constructed from the mathematics of Sir Isaac Newton and others, the view was developed that the human mind was all-sufficient and there was no need for an external source of knowledge or inspiration such as God. This humanistic view came to prevail in intellectual circles, leaving little room for God. For a time He was tolerated on the periphery of human experience. Deism was a movement that saw God as a watchmaker. He created the world, the solar system, and the universe—then wound it up so that it would run on its own, according to its own laws that scientists were discovering.

Soon, however, the theory of evolution came along in the mid-nineteenth century and removed God from even that small role. Now there was no longer any need for a watchmaker to make the watch in the first place. The watch had evolved on its own. All of this led to a direct confrontation between the biblical school of thought and rationalistic humanism. The Bible says there is a God and that He has revealed Himself. Rationalistic humanism says there is no God, and there is no revelation from Him. The Bible thus becomes central to this debate.

One aspect of the Bible that demonstrates that there is a God and that He has revealed Himself is the matter of predictive prophecy. It might be that an especially well-informed person could accurately guess the course of events in the immediate or near future. But to propose that someone, utilizing only natural human resources, could correctly predict what was going to happen five, six, or seven centuries in advance, as is the case in the book of Daniel, goes far beyond any natural human knowledge. Such insight could come only from the realm of the supernatural. As a consequence, the issue of predictive prophecy has played a significant part in discussions between those who accept the biblical view and those who do not.

Those who deny the biblical view of God and history must find a humanistic explanation for the predictive aspect of the prophecies given in the Bible. One way to nullify the predictive content of a prophetic book such as Daniel is to say that its prophecies were not fulfilled, that the events predicted did not come to pass. Later chapters of this book will take up the evidences for the fulfillment of the prophecies of Daniel.

But there is another way to cancel the predictive element of a prophetic book, and that is to demonstrate that the book's local historical content is inaccurate. For example, Daniel's prophecies purport to have been given in the setting of sixth-century B.C. Babylon. If Daniel, supposedly writing from the vantage point of sixth-century B.C. Babylon, does not have his Babylonian history straight, then one need not give credence to any of the prophetic details he gives either. In other words, one way to undermine the prophetic section of Daniel is to first undermine the accuracy of its historical section. If the historical accuracy of the book can be impugned, its prophecies need not be taken seriously.

But if this argument has validity, then the reverse must also be valid. If we can demonstrate that Daniel's historical sections *are* accurate and dependable, then we must take seriously what he says in the prophetic sections as well. We turn, then, to that issue—the historical accuracy of Daniel.

The Historical Accuracy of Daniel

Those who do not accept the view that God is intimately involved in human history and who have no place in their thinking for predictive prophecy, have pointed to a number of supposed historical inaccuracies in Daniel's book as a means of denying the predictive element of the prophetic portions. So the problem for those who see Daniel's prophetic portions as predicting events far in the future is to meet these objections and demonstrate the historical accuracy of the book. We will do this by taking up five of the major objections that have been raised against the historical accuracy of Daniel. There is evidence in each of these cases to indicate that rather than being historical inaccuracies in the biblical record, they are actually misunderstandings by modern historians of what the record really says.

However, before we take up these five individual objections to the historical accuracy of Daniel, let's examine the basic presuppositions that underlie them as a whole.

Scholars who study Daniel from the viewpoint of rationalistic humanism cannot accommodate supernatural revelation into their understanding of the book. Such a view, of course, excludes the possibility that Daniel's prophecies were actually given in the sixth century B.C. and predicted subsequent events centuries in the future. The usual explanation has been that the book of Daniel was actually written much later—most probably in the second century B.C. The writer is supposed to have been an anonymous individual who lived in Jerusalem in 165 B.C., during the time of Antiochus IV Epiphanes, a Greek king from Syria. Antiochus IV persecuted the Jews and disrupted their religious services in the temple, so much of the prophecy in Daniel is thought to focus upon him and his persecuting activities. Thus, these scholars argue, the so-called prophecies of Daniel are really history written in the form of prophecy. That is, a second-century B.C. writer based his material on contemporary events taking place around him, but presented them in the form of prophecies that purported to have been written in the sixth century B.C. predicting these events.

And if the writer of Daniel actually lived in the second century B.C., naturally he would not be able to present the history of sixth-century B.C. Babylon without making mistakes. Thus, according to this argument, inaccuracies in the history of Babylon and the sixth century B.C. are proof of a late authorship for the book and the lack of a true predictive element in the prophecies.

Let's turn, then, to the five major examples that have been cited as historical inaccuracies in the book of Daniel. What is the evidence? Are these indeed historical mistakes—or misunderstandings on the part of the critics?

1. The Date in Daniel 1:1

Daniel 1:1 gives the date of Nebuchadnezzar's first siege of Jerusalem as "in the third year of the reign of Jehoiakim king of Judah." Critical scholars argue that the correct date is actually the *fourth* year of Jehoiakim, or 605 B.C., when correlated with the events described in Nebuchadnezzar's own chronicles.

The sequence of events runs like this: Josiah, King of Judah, died when he went out to fight Pharaoh Neco at Megiddo in the summer of 609 B.C., as the Egyptian ruler was on his way north to fight with the Babylonians (see 2 Kings 23:29). An accurate date for this campaign of Neco can be obtained from the Babylonian Chronicle, the official record of the first eleven years of Nebuchadnezzar's reign. Upon his return from northern Syria in the fall of that same year, Neco deposed Jehoahaz of Judah and carried him off to Egypt (see 2 Kings 23:33-35). In his place he installed Jehoiakim as king (verse 34).

The important chronological point here is that this final transition, the installation of Jehoiakim as Judah's king, took place after Rosh Hashanah, the fall New Year. Thus the first official year of Jehoiakim's reign began in the fall of 608 B.C. The period of time before that fall New Year was known as the "accession year" or Year 0. Thus Jehoiakim's third year, mentioned in Daniel 1:1, began in the fall of 606 B.C. and extended to the fall of 605 B.C. Within that year, Nebuchadnezzar fought the battle of Carchemish in Syria in the spring (Jeremiah 46:2). He came up to Jerusalem in the summer of that year before Jehoiakim's fourth year began in the fall.

Thus if one interprets this date according to the principle of accession year reckoning and the Jewish (fall-to-fall) calendar, the date works out correctly as the Jewish fall-to-fall year of 606/605 B.C., which is historically accurate.

2. Belshazzar as King of Babylon

Another criticism of the historical episodes in the book of Daniel has centered around the figure of Belshazzar in chapter 5. It is clear from various historical sources that the last king of the Neo-Babylonian Empire was Nabonidus, not Belshazzar. Yet Daniel 5 portrays Belshazzar as the king in the palace of Babylon the night the city fell to the Persians.

Knowledge about the existence of Belshazzar was lost from the time of the ancient world down to the year 1861 A.D. During those years, he was unknown from primary historical sources, and various theories were advanced about his identity, especially during the eighteenth and nineteenth centuries A.D. In 1861 the first cuneiform tablet was published mentioning Belshazzar by name. Twenty years later, Nabonidus' Chronicle was published; it told about a series of years during which Belshazzar managed governmental affairs in Babylon while his father Nabonidus was in Arabia. Finally, in 1924, another cuneiform text was published, now called the Verse Account of Nabonidus. It tells, among other things, that when Nabonidus left Babylon, he "entrusted the kingship" to his son Belshazzar. Thus a whole interconnected series of tablets have been discovered in recent years which reveal the role that Belshazzar played in political and military events of Babylon in the sixth century B.C.

On this point, the critics of Daniel's history have had to retreat. One wrote candidly, "Presumably we shall never know how the author of Daniel knew of these events." Actually, it is easy to understand when one takes the evidence of the book itself into account. The answer is that Daniel was on the scene of action at the time as an eyewitness.

Still trying to rescue some credibility from this turn of events, critics have exploited another aspect of this problem. They have noted that there is no specific Babylonian tablet which directly refers to Belshazzar as "king." This observation is accurate as far as it goes. But what does it mean when the Verse Account of Nabonidus says he "entrusted the kingship" to Belshazzar?

A Hebrew who came out of the political environment Daniel did would be well aware of the practice of co-regency. David put Solomon on the throne with him so that there were two co-kings ruling Israel for a time. This also happened again at various times in Israel's history. Daniel, therefore, simply referred to Belshazzar as "king" because he occupied the position of king and functioned as a king. Daniel was historically correct because he knew who was ruling in

Babylon while Nabonidus was away from the capital for ten years.

There is a small, but important, detail in Daniel 5 that shows just how accurate Daniel's knowledge of Belshazzar and his fate really was. Daniel tells us who was in the palace in the city that night—and who was not. Belshazzar was there, but Nabonidus, the chief king, was not. This detail is something that could have been known only by a witness to those events in the sixth century B.C. A writer in the second century B.C. might well have made the mistake of putting Nabonidus, the last chief king, in the palace that night. But Daniel did not make that mistake, and the Nabonidus Chronicle tells us where Nabonidus was. He had taken one division of the Babylonian army out to the Tigris River to fight Cyrus and his troops as they approached from the east. Belshazzar was left in the city with the other division to protect it. The writer of Daniel knew that Belshazzar was in the city the night it fell, and he makes no mention of Nabonidus for the obvious reason that he was elsewhere. This small, seemingly insignificant, detail reveals just how historically accurate Daniel was in the case of Belshazzar.

3. The Separate Median Kingdom

For centuries, orthodox interpreters of the book of Daniel have seen its fourfold sequence of kingdoms in chapters 2 and 7 as representing Babylon, Medo-Persia, Greece, and Rome. Since the book of Daniel mentions a king named Darius *the Mede*, critical scholars have argued that the writer of Daniel thought there was a separate Median kingdom *after* the Babylonian kingdom. Therefore, they feel that on the evidence of the book itself, the sequence should be shortened to Babylon, Media, Persia, and Greece. In this way the series ends not with Rome, but with Antiochus Epiphanes who came out of the Greek kingdom. This, they say, is consistent with what a second-century B.C. author would write, but that it is a historical mistake to speak of a separate Median kingdom after the time of Babylon.

There *was* a separate Median kingdom back in the ninth, eighth, and seventh centuries B.C. That is well known and is not at issue. But the critics are correct that it would be a historical error to insert a separate Median kingdom in this sequence *after* 539 B.C. when the Babylonian kingdom fell. The Medes had been conquered by the Persians earlier in the sixth century B.C. and for the next two centuries were an integral component of the Persian Empire.

Did the writer of Daniel make such a mistake and identify a separate kingdom of Media? Not on the basis of the evidence in the text. The ram in the prophecy of chapter 8 is identified in verse 20: "the two-horned ram that you saw represents the kings of Media and Persia." The single symbolic ram represented the single kingdom of Medo-Persia.

The same point is made in the narrative of chapter 6 where the law given by Darius was said to be "in accordance with the laws of the Medes and Persians, which cannot be repealed" (vs. 12). If Media and Persia were separate kingdoms at this time, the reference would have been to "the laws of the Medes and the laws of the Persians" rather than to "the laws of the Medes and Persians." One codex of laws governed the dual kingdom.

The writing on the wall in 5:28 teaches the same thing, for Belshazzar's kingdom was "divided and given to the Medes and Persians." There are no grounds in the book of Daniel for separating an individual Median kingdom. The sequence should stand as it has been interpreted—Babylon, Medo-Persia, Greece, and Rome.

4. Darius the Mede

The identity of Darius the Mede is still a matter of some dispute even among conservative scholars who accept his historical existence. This case is not yet as clear as the one that deals with Belshazzar. Several candidates have been mentioned as possibilities, including two Persian kings, two Median kings, and two Persian governors. These will be discussed in more detail in the chapter that deals with Daniel 6. Here only two points need to be mentioned.

First, we know there was a coregent in Babylon during the first year of Persian control. The everyday, business tablets of Babylon at this time carry the names of the kings and their titles, along with a date expressed in terms of the king's regnal year. From these documents, it is clear that Cyrus did not carry the title "King of Babylon" for the first year after the Persian conquest; none of the tablets written then assign that title to him.

Second, there is the matter of throne names. In ancient times, kings commonly had personal names before they took the throne; after taking the kingship, they assumed another official name. This was very common in Egypt and was practiced occasionally in Israel. Azariah, who was also named Uzziah, is an example. This custom was used rarely in Mesopotamia, but perhaps somewhat more commonly in Persia, according to some modern historians. Thus Darius, as mentioned in Daniel, could well be a throne name, but we still need to be more accurate in identifying the personal name of the individual who may have taken that throne name.

5. The Date of Daniel's Aramaic Language

Earlier studies argued that the Aramaic language used in chapters 2–7 of Daniel more closely matched the Aramaic of the second century B.C., than that of the sixth century B.C. However, when those studies were carried out, only one set of ancient Aramaic texts was well known—the Elephantine Papyri from fifth-century B.C. Egypt. Since Daniel's Aramaic differed somewhat from the language used in the Elephantine Papyri, it was argued that Daniel's Aramaic was from a later period.

A steady stream of discoveries of Aramaic inscriptions has since given us a much more complete picture of that language and its development—and a better basis of comparison with the Aramaic appearing in Daniel. The differences between the Aramaic of Daniel and that found in the Elephantine Papyri were thought at one time to represent a chronological development in this language but are now known to be a regional dialect development instead. The Elephantine Papyri that formed the original basis for comparison all came from Egypt and reflected an Egyptian dialect of Aramaic. This dialect differed from the way the language was written and spoken in Judah, Syria, Babylonia, and Iran. Each of these regions had its own regional dialect. A number of the Aramaic features in the book of Daniel that were thought to be late characteristics—such as the position of the verb, for example—are now known to be early characteristics peculiar to eastern regions, in other words, like the Aramaic of Babylonia where Daniel lived!

Another major development in this area has come from the discovery of the Dead Sea Scrolls. The Essenes who worked at the monastery at Qumran by the Dead Sea from the second century B.C. to the late first century A.D. wrote and copied a number of Aramaic documents, as well as Hebrew texts. As these documents have been published, it has become clear that Daniel's Aramaic is considerably older than these Dead Sea documents. Since modern critical scholars believe Daniel was written at about the same time as the Dead Sea Scrolls, it is awkward for their view that there is not a closer correspondence in terms of language. The Aramaic Dead Sea scrolls have also revealed that Daniel's Aramaic is not Palestinian by geographic distribution. Rather, it is an eastern type of Aramaic, as one would expect of a resident of Babylonia.

Thus the major developments in the study of the Aramaic language appearing in Daniel have all tended to move the date for that writing earlier than the critics believed. At present, Daniel's Aramaic is simply classified as "Imperial Aramaic," meaning that it fits well within the dates of the Persian Empire from the seventh through the fourth centuries B.C. The linguistic argument is no longer a serviceable argument against the earlier date of Daniel's Aramaic.

Thus after examining the major objections to the historical accuracy of Daniel, we can say with assurance that its language and historical content corroborate the testimony of the book itself, that it was written in the sixth century B.C. Thus the argument of the critics, that we cannot trust its prophetic statements because of its historical inaccuracies, is shattered.

The Literary Structure of the Historical Chapters

In concluding this chapter, we need to look at one other feature of the first half of the book. This feature does not have to do with dating or determining historicity; rather, it deals with why the chapters of Daniel are arranged in the order in which they are.

The careful reader will realize that the historical narratives of the book are not arranged in a strictly chronological order. For example, chapters 5 and 6, which are dated in the Persian period, precede chapters 7 and 8, which belong to the earlier Babylonian period. A chronological order would require that chapters 7 and 8 should precede chapters 5 and 6. So some other organizing principle must have been used. As noted earlier, Daniel does divide—with some overlap—into roughly equal sections of historical and prophetic chapters.

More than that, however, the chapters that were written in Aramaic—chapters 2 through 7—exhibit a specific literary order. These six chapters stand apart from the rest of the book on the basis of the language used. They also stand apart in terms of literary structure—the way they are ordered within their own section. These chapters are clearly related to each other in pairs, based on content. Chapters 2 and 7 form one pair; both chapters are outline prophecies that deal with the rise and fall of kingdoms over great portions of human history.

Likewise, chapters 3 and 6 are also similar in content. Chapter 3 describes the persecution of Daniel's three friends in the fiery furnace; chapter 6 describes Daniel's own persecution in the lions' den. In both cases God's servants suffer trials for their faith, and in both cases they are supernaturally delivered from those trials.

This leaves chapters 4 and 5 standing together as a pair within the Aramaic and historical portion of the book. These chapters also deal with the same subject—an individual Babylonian king. In chapter 4, it is Nebuchadnezzar who is in view. In chapter 5, it is Belshazzar. Both of these narratives begin with a local setting—Nebuchadnezzar in his palace, and Belshazzar in that same palace. Both of these kings had become cases of vaunted ego, and both were judged by the true God. In both instances, their judgments came in the form of prophecies which were subsequently fulfilled. Daniel was present to interpret both of these prophecies. The two stories have slightly different endings, but even here, they still bear a relationship to each other. In chapter 4, Nebuchadnezzar fell into a period of insanity but then was able to rise again and return to his throne. In chapter 5, however, there is no subsequent redemption for Belshazzar. He and his city fell that night to the Persian conquerors.

Thus the narratives of the Aramaic and historical section of the book of Daniel line up according to thematic pairs along the following kind of outline:

A. Daniel 2—prophecy about the rise and fall of kingdoms
   B. Daniel 3—narrative about the persecution of Daniel's friends
      C. Daniel 4—prophecy about fall and rise of King Nebuchadnezzar
      C. Daniel 5—prophecy about the fall of King Belshazzar
   B. Daniel 6—narrative about the persecution of Daniel
A. Daniel 7—prophecy about the rise and fall of kingdoms

Such an outline is like a stepladder with steps on both sides in which one ascends in the same order that one descends the steps on the other side—A : B : C : C : B : A. The technical name for this order of writing is a *chiasm*. This word comes from the name of the Greek letter *chi*, which looks something like an X. The idea is that the outline proceeds up one leg of this kind of X and then follows in reverse order down the other. It is organization based on inversion, or a mirror image. What we have here in Daniel is a relatively simple *chiasm* based upon thematic links between two stories of a similar nature. A glance at the chiastic outline above shows that chapters 2 and 7 are thematically linked, as are chapters 3 and 6 and chapters 4 and 5. This kind of arrangement is fairly common in the Old Testament, especially in the psalms, so it is evident that the people of Daniel's time were well aware of this type of writing.

What purpose did it serve for them, and what value does it have for us today? It served several functions. First, it was an easy memory device. If you had to memorize the contents of these six chapters of Daniel, that might be a difficult assignment. However, it would be much easier to remember what each chapter is about once you recognize this inverse order.

Second, this kind of organization makes it possible to see explanatory links between the paired narratives. For example, many commentators have recognized that the prophecy of chapter 7 is a further and more detailed explanation of the prophecy given in chapter 2. The two prophecies are related; they are not referring to different and distinct periods of history. The literary structure, then, becomes simply another way to reinforce that link.

Third, there is the matter of aesthetics. It is good to recognize that the Bible speaks to us in many different ways and cultures. But it is also good to realize that there is literary beauty in these expressions as well. We recognize the literary beauty of some of the psalms. Why not recognize the literary beauty of some biblical prose, such as these chapters in Daniel? Daniel is not the small, insignificant work of an unimportant editor; this is the work, under God, of a literary artist, and we need to recognize his skill.

Finally, this literary structure emphasizes the unity of this section of Daniel and the whole book. These narratives have been very precisely fitted together in a specific order, like the bricks used to build a fireplace. One cannot be removed without having the whole structure crumble. Each is vital to the order and relationship. Literary critics of Daniel have missed this point. They have tried to separate chapter 7 from the rest of the historical chapters. For them, the prophecy of chapter 7 was written about 165 B.C. in the time of Antiochus Epiphanes, but the preceding historical chapters were written earlier, they say, perhaps in the fourth or third centuries B.C. But these narratives, embedded as they are in this literary architecture, cannot be so easily dismembered. Chapter 7 belongs with chapter 2; the two are a pair. And that pair forms a frame around the other four chapters that have been paired together. Thus the historical chapters are all a unit, a package, and the fact that they were also all written in the same Aramaic language emphasizes that point. For a century and a half, source critics have been breaking up Daniel into smaller and smaller pieces. Finally, an appreciation of the literary artistry and structure of the book has demonstrated how wrong such an approach has been. The book of Daniel is one literary unit, and an aesthetically attractive one at that.

Because of this unique literary structure of the historical section of Daniel, we will study these chapters in the pairs to which they belong.

For Further Reading

1. For a brief and concise history of Babylon, see G. Roux, *Ancient Iraq.*

2. For a fuller and more detailed history of Babylon, see H. W. F. Saggs, *The Greatness That Was Babylon.*

3. For details about the city of Babylon, see S. H. Horn, *The Spade Confirms the Book.*

4. For discussions of the problems of Belshazzar in Daniel 5 and Darius the Mede in Daniel 6, see the special studies on these problems in F. D. Nichol, ed., *The Seventh-day Adventist Bible Commentary*, vol. 4, 806-808, 814-817.

5. For an evangelical study of some of the historical and linguistic problems in the book of Daniel, see D. J. Wiseman, et al., *Notes on Some Problems in the Book of Daniel.*

CHAPTER TWO

Exiled

Daniel 1

With the exception of a small part of the first chapter, the entire book of Daniel is set in Babylon. That is because Daniel lived there most of his adult life, and he lived a long time. The first date in the book, at the beginning of chapter 1, is equivalent to 605 B.C. in our calendar. The last date, the date that accompanies the last prophecy of the book (Daniel 10:1), is equivalent to 536 B.C. That gives us a span of almost seventy years that Daniel spent in Babylon. During most of this time he lived under Neo-Babylonian kings, but he spent the very last years of his life under the Persian kings who conquered Babylon. Daniel probably died soon after receiving the last prophecy recorded in his book. In fact, when the angel Gabriel gave him that prophecy, he appears to have indicated to Daniel that that would soon be the case.

Daniel was probably in early adulthood when he was taken to Babylon. Some have suggested that he was perhaps around eighteen years of age, an age that would fit well with Babylonian policy for captives. Thus of the almost ninety years that Daniel lived, he spent approximately the first twenty in Judah and the last seventy in Babylon. Living so long in Babylon meant that Daniel was well acquainted with the city and the nation, its rulers, and its procedures at court. He came to Nebuchadnezzar's court soon after his exile and probably served there a long time, since Nebuchadnezzar enjoyed a lengthy rulership of forty-three years, and Daniel seems to have held an important position in public service at least during Nebuchadnezzar's lifetime. After the death of Nebuchadnezzar, however, Daniel appears to have fallen from favor of the later rulers of Babylon. It was not until the very last of these, Belshazzar, that Daniel was rehabili-

tated to his former position of prominence, and then only briefly. But his popularity continued into the Persian period when he also achieved some prominence, though at the cost of considerable difficulty to himself.

In good times or in bad, Daniel was a model of faithfulness and perseverance. He was also a model in his constant and dedicated devotional life, though this too came at a considerable cost to himself. Daniel is, therefore, a bright example to us of one who had courage, loyalty to his God, perseverance, and a living communion with that God. Since several of his prophecies close with the time of the end in which we now live, Daniel's example in these areas is an excellent reminder for us that we, too, should live for God in spite of the circumstances, good or bad, we may encounter.

As a person who lived in Babylon for many years and who also worked at its power center, Daniel obviously knew Babylon very well. Prophets of God may speak to the distant future on occasion, as Daniel did. But they also spoke to their own times and people. For Daniel, that was Babylon in the sixth century B.C. and the people of God who lived in exile there. It is only natural, therefore, that Babylon and its history would play a prominent part in the prophecies that God gave to him. Babylon appears in no less than four of the prophecies God gave to Daniel—appearing in chapters 2, 4, 5, and 7 of the book. A knowledge of Babylon and its history in the seventh and sixth centuries B.C. should be of use to us, then, in terms of understanding the prophet in the context of the time and place in which he lived. Such an understanding serves as a jumping off point for the successive steps in the prophecies which God has revealed to us through Daniel.

■ Getting Into the Word

Daniel 1

Read Daniel 1 through at least two times. Then respond to the following exercises:

1. **With the help of a concordance, discover what you can about Jehoiakim and his reign. Summarize your findings in a paragraph or two. Compare your findings with the article on Jehoiakim in a Bible dictionary.**

2. Discover what you can about Nebuchadnezzar by following the suggestions given for Jehoiakim in the previous exercise.

3. As further background for studying the book of Daniel, examine the articles on "Babylon" and "Captivity" or "Babylonian Captivity" in a Bible dictionary. In what ways can the information in those articles help you understand the book of Daniel?

4. What light does Deuteronomy 28:1–30:20 shed on the reason for the captivity of God's chosen people?

5. What specific things can you learn about Daniel as a person by reading chapter 1? List them in your notebook. What can you learn from this chapter about the Babylonians' treatment of Daniel? List these as well. What do you think the Babylonians had in mind for Daniel and his companions? Explain why you think the Babylonians had such care for these captives.

6. Summarize in your own words the food and drink issue in Daniel 1. What was the problem with the king's food and drink? For a partial answer to that question, you may want to examine such texts as Leviticus 11, Deuteronomy 14:1-21, and Leviticus 17:10-14.

7. What do you think Daniel and his friends studied in the "University of Babylon"? A reading of Daniel 2 will provide some hints. Look up some of the areas of expertise (such as astrology and magic) of Babylon's educated class in a Bible dictionary. Why do you think Daniel may have rejected the king's food but not the king's learning?

8. List the indications of divine guidance and/or divine providence in Daniel 1.

■ Exploring the Word

Daniel's Times

One way of looking at Daniel is to suggest that he was a merely a small pawn who got caught up in the international power politics of his time. Such an evaluation has to do with the shifting politics and loyalties in the late seventh century B.C.

It was a time of transition. Judah existed on a narrow strip of land between the Mediterranean Sea and the eastern desert. That narrow corridor of land stood squarely in the path of conquest for both the Egyptians to the south and the Mesopotamian powers of Assyria and Babylon to the north. Repeatedly, powerful military forces from the north and the south pushed through Palestine. (See the map of the ancient Near East on page 53.) In rapid succession, the little kingdom of Judah came under the control of three different nations in the late seventh century B.C.

First, there was Assyria. Ashurbanipal, the last great king of the Assyrian empire, died in 626 B.C., just two or three years before Daniel was born. With his death, major changes took place in the Near East. The Assyrian empire broke up into many pieces, and for a time the people of Judah enjoyed a respite as Assyrian control was weakened. King Josiah took the opportunity of that interval to begin a religious reformation in the country (see 2 Kings 22:8–23:25). As the prophet Jeremiah indicated, however, Josiah's reform did not go deep enough or last long enough.

In this power vacuum, the aggressive pharaohs of the twenty-sixth dynasty in Egypt soon moved into position to take control of Western Asia as far as the Euphrates River where they held sway for approximately a decade. Meanwhile, a new power was rising in the east. The Babylonians, joining with the Medes from the mountains of northern Iran, successfully attacked the major population centers of Assyria—Nimrud and Nineveh. They conquered these cities and then destroyed them. As they moved up the eastern branch of the Euphrates, their activities brought them into confrontation with the Egyptians in the area of the upper river.

After an initial skirmish in 611 B.C., the Babylonians and Egyptians fought a major battle in 605 B.C. Jeremiah mentions this battle in Jeremiah 46:1-12, where he provides a view of the disastrous defeat of the Egyptians. We also have the words of Nebuchadnezzar's own royal annals for these events. There his scribe recorded:

Nebuchadnezzar his [Nabopolassar's] eldest son, the crown prince, mustered [the Babylonian army] and took command of

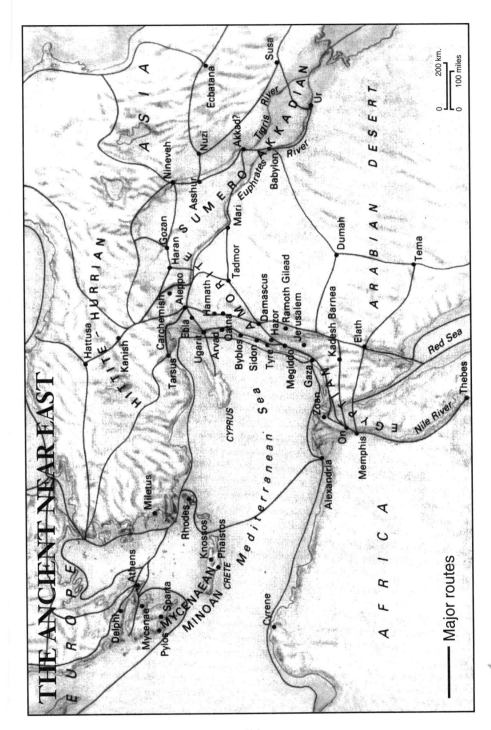

THE ANCIENT NEAR EAST

EUROPE

ASIA

HITTITE

HURRIAN

SUMERO-AKKADIAN

ARAM

CANAAN

EGYPT

AFRICA

ARABIAN DESERT

Mediterranean Sea

CYPRUS

CRETE

MINOAN

MYCENAEAN

Red Sea

Nile River

Tigris River

Euphrates River

Babylon River

Delphi
Athens
Mycenae
Sparta
Pylos
Miletus
Rhodes
Knossos
Phaistos
Cyrene
Alexandria
Memphis
On
Zoan
Thebes
Gaza
Megiddo
Jerusalem
Kadesh Barnea
Elath
Ramoth Gilead
Hazor
Tyre
Sidon
Byblos
Arvad
Damascus
Qatna
Ugarit
Hamath
Ebla
Aleppo
Tarsus
Carchemish
Kanish
Hattusa
Gozan
Haran
Tadmor
Mari
Nineveh
Nuzi
Akkad?
Asshur
Ecbatana
Susa
Ur
Dumah
Tema

0   200 km.
0   100 miles

—— Major routes

53

his troops; he marched to Carchemish which is on the bank of the Euphrates, and crossed the river [to go] against the Egyptian army which lay in Carchemish, . . . [they] fought with each other and the Egyptian army withdrew before him. He accomplished their defeat and beat them to non-existence.

These decisive events turned the whole political landscape of the ancient Near East upside down. What had formerly been under the control of Egypt now came under the control of Babylon, including all the territory south to the border of Egypt. Quite naturally, that included the kingdom of Judah. Royal records from Babylon—the Babylonian Chronicle texts—illuminate this situation. These texts, written in cuneiform, or wedge-shaped writing on clay tablets, were year-by-year accounts of the major events during the reign of the king. They do not give details for this particular conquest but state in general terms: "At that time Nebuchadnezzar conquered the whole area of Hatti-country." The designation "Hatti-country" was a hold-over from the days when the Hittites ruled Syria and Palestine. The Hittites were long since gone, but the designation still remained. It included all the kingdoms from Syria in the north to Judah in the south.

One may ask why Nebuchadnezzar's records did not specifically mention Jerusalem as one of the cities he conquered. The probable reason was because Jehoiakim, the king of Judah at the time, could see that resistance to Nebuchadnezzar was futile, and he surrendered. Thus it wasn't necessary for the Babylonians to mount a full-scale war against the city. The Babylonian Chronicle texts mention only those cities which held out until Babylonian troops overran them. Cities which surrendered before that point, like Jerusalem, were not mentioned by name.

An observer of the historical scene in the Near East in 605 B.C. might have thought that all of this was merely the result of shifting human loyalties and power. But there was more to it than that. Daniel indicates this additional dimension at the very beginning of his book. Jehoiakim surrendered and fell into the hands of Nebuchadnezzar not just because he was a bad king, which he was, but because God permitted and directed events in this way. There was an unseen factor involved in the course of these events, and that factor was a divine one. Daniel 1:2 says, "And the Lord delivered Jehoiakim king of Judah into his hand." While this was not God's original intent for His people, their apostasy—led by King Jehoiakim—brought about this sad course of events. Since God's people had relinquished their faith in Him and had given up participating in His covenant, they had also forfeited His protection from enemies such as Babylon (see Deuteronomy 28:1–30:20).

Daniel's Personal Experience

Even though a vigorous faith in the true God was largely lacking in Judah at this time, there still were those who were faithful to God. Daniel and his friends were among those who held on to their faith in spite of the generally prevailing apostasy. This did not prevent them from being taken into exile, but it did give them the opportunity to witness for their faith during that exile. In fact, the faithfulness of these servants of God in even the most trying of times is one of the bright spots in the book of Daniel. The question comes to us then: Do we meet similar, or even lesser, trials in our lives with a corresponding measure of faith? With such a strong example of courage and faith left for us by Daniel and his friends, should we not exercise the same devotion and trust in God to meet the trials that come to us?

Imagine yourself in Daniel's situation. You are young, just on the verge of beginning your adult life. Every opportunity seems to stretch before you. But then a sudden curve in the pathway of experience appears before you. Instead of being able to take advantage of the opportunities in your own home city and country, you are dragged off to a foreign land quite remote from your own. Further, you are given no privileges in your journey and have to walk four hundred miles across the desert to get to your destination. You have no assurance that you will ever see your home or family again. In fact, it looks very much as though you will not. What would your attitude have been? Discouragement? Depression? Would you have questioned how God could have done all this to you? Now that no one from your homeland could see you, would you have decided that you might as well live any way you could to get along in the land of your captors?

Some of these ideas may well have passed through the minds of Daniel and his friends, but they gave them no permanent heed in reacting to their difficult circumstances.

Taking hostages from captive countries was standard policy exercised by both the Babylonians and the Egyptians. Young men of considerable potential were taken back to the heartland of the empire to be trained in Babylonian or Egyptian ways and culture. This was done for a purpose. The point was to train these young men for future service to the empire. When the current king or administrators of the captive countries passed off the scene of action, their places could be taken by natives of those countries who had now been trained in Babylonian or Egyptian thinking. In that way Babylon, for example, could obtain administrators who had an intimate knowledge of the local customs of the people whom they governed, but who would have their ultimate loyalties cultivated toward Babylon through their education.

When Daniel and his friends arrived in Babylon, they began an extensive course of study. The different disciplines which they mastered were to enable them to become better Babylonian bureaucrats, better government servants. They undoubtedly studied the Babylonian cuneiform writing. This involved learning an elaborate system of signs to be incised upon soft clay with a pointed stylus. Cuneiform writing has provided us with some of the oldest samples of writing produced by the human race. Many examples have survived the centuries and with good reason—when the clay hardened, it provided a relatively permanent record. If the records were very important, such as state documents of a king, the cuneiform tablets involved were fired in a kiln. This hardened them even more than drying in the sun and made them very durable, much more durable than the paper we use today. If the records were not so important, they were left to dry naturally and harden more gradually. These less durable tablets were more easily broken, which is why excavators digging in ancient Near Eastern ruins often find many more fragments than whole tablets. It takes careful work in a museum to piece together those fragments of tablets that belong together.

Even though the Babylonian writing system was cumbersome to learn, the language itself probably was not very difficult for Daniel and his friends. Babylonian belongs to what is known as the East Semitic language family, while Hebrew belongs to the West Semitic group. Both are in the same general language family, and it would not have been very difficult for Daniel and his friends to pick up the Babylonian language. In addition, some of the work at the Babylonian court was done in Aramaic, a language even closer to Hebrew.

Nebuchadnezzar himself was not a native-born Babylonian in the ethnic and cultural sense. He, and his father Nabopolassar before him, belonged to one of the tribes of the Chaldean people who lived in southern Babylonia. These tribes spoke Aramaic, thus Nebuchadnezzar's own native tongue would have been Aramaic. It was quite natural, therefore, for Daniel to converse with Nebuchadnezzar in this language and for several of the dialogues between these two individuals to be recorded in Aramaic. This provides a partial explanation why the book of Daniel was written in two languages—chapters 1, 8–12 in Hebrew and chapters 2–7 in Aramaic.

We know a lot about the sciences as they were studied and practiced in Babylon. Those durable clay tablets have provided us with many of the Babylonians' astronomical calculations and their system of mathematics. Our modern system of mathematics is based upon units of ten, the decimal system. But the Babylonian system was based on units of six, known as sexagesimal mathematics. Some of this system has come down to us today; it explains why there are sixty seconds in a minute, sixty minutes in an hour, and 360 degrees in a circle. The Babylonian system shows up in Daniel 3 where the measurements of the image that Nebuchadnezzar set up—sixty cubits high and six cubits wide—are given in typical Babylonian sexagesimal measurements.

One of the more unpleasant problems the Hebrews faced in their Babylonian curriculum was the subject of astrology. The scientific side of that subject is astronomy, and that was not a problem. The interpretive, subjective side of this subject, however, is astrology. Babylonian culture was steeped in this sort of thing, and the Hebrew captives were probably introduced to it in their classes.

Here we find a sharp, distinct difference between the Bible and the ancient world. The ancient world was much devoted to the subject of astrology, observations based on the motions of the heavenly bodies used to predict human events and their outcomes. The Bible, however, is diametrically opposed to this sort of thing. This opposition is clearly stated in both Mosaic legislation (see Deuteronomy 18:9-14), and by the prophets (see Isaiah 8:19, 20). In this respect, therefore, the Bible stands diametrically opposed to some of the practices that went on in the environment surrounding the Israelites. Daniel and his friends would undoubtedly have opposed the use of these astrological methods in their work for the government of Babylon. They had a source upon which to rely for a knowledge of the future that was much more sure than the divination practices of Babylon. That source was the true God.

It is a paradox, therefore, that Daniel was eventually placed in charge of the wise men of Babylon (2:48) who were active practitioners of astrology. Some of the episodes described later in his book demonstrate the superiority of the knowledge received from the true God as opposed to the false methods of the wise men (see chaps. 2–4).

Although we agree with Daniel's opposition to the thoughts and practices of Babylonian religion, we should also be fair to the Babylonians in terms of what they did and did not try to do with these captives. This issue comes up in terms of the names that were assigned to the Hebrews. Once he arrived in the capital, Daniel was given the new name of Belteshazzar (1:7). This is a sentence which breaks down into three components: *Belit*, the title of a goddess; *shar*, the word for "king"; and the verb *uzur*, which means "to protect." Literally, therefore, Daniel's Babylonian name means, "May [the goddess] Belit protect the king." The Babylonian ruler, Belshazzar, carried a very similar name, the only difference being that the title of Bel, "lord," referred to a masculine rather than a feminine deity.

Daniel's three friends were given similar names that conveyed meaning, and that meaning was, in some cases, connected with Babylonian gods. This does not mean, however, that the Babylonians were trying to forcibly convert Daniel and his friends to the Babylonian religion simply by giving them names which contained a divine element. The goal was much more pragmatic than that. The Babylonians simply wanted to give these captives names which would be easy to recognize by the Babylonians with whom they would be working.

The Test

Soon after enrolling in the scribal school in Babylon, Daniel and his three friends ran into trouble. The trouble was not over astrology or their Babylonian names or worshiping idols. It was over food. Students complaining about the food they are served at school is not a modern phenomenon; it goes back a long way, 2,500 years in this case! But in this instance there were excellent grounds for lodging the complaint: "Daniel resolved not to defile himself with the royal food and wine, and he asked the chief official for permission not to defile himself this way" (1:8).

The question arises, Why did Daniel refuse to eat the food that was provided from the royal quartermaster depot or kitchen? The text gives us a very clear and direct answer: "Daniel resolved not to defile himself."

It would have been an interesting conversation to listen to as Daniel was trying to explain to the Babylonian official this defilement based upon the dietary laws set out in Leviticus 11 and Deuteronomy 14! Among the cuneiform texts which have been cataloged and translated are some which list the foodstuffs that were provided to the Babylonian army. Supplies included pork. For an Israelite, pork was unclean and considered unfit to eat. If pork was supplied to the army in the field, it probably was supplied to the bureaucrats in the palace and to students in the scribal school. Thus Daniel and his friends would have had to face the issue of unclean meat being served to them. This they declined to eat because it would "defile" them.

Other reasons were probably involved as well. As in the New Testament case at Corinth, some of the meat provided in Babylon may have been offered to idols (see 1 Corinthians 8). Then, too, there was the matter of the preparation of the food. Babylonian butchers would not have prepared any of their meats in a way that would have been considered kosher for a Jew (see Leviticus 17:10-14). The preparation could also have involved highly spiced foods.

The easiest and most direct way to avoid all of these problems was to eat a vegetarian diet and drink only water. That is what Daniel requested of the official. Literally, he asked for "seed-food," that which grows from seeds, or plant food (1:12). Daniel could see the problems involved in the Babylonian diet, and he could also see that the most direct way to avoid them was to avoid the problem altogether rather than to try to eat his way around it. He asked for a vegetarian diet and the principal nonalcoholic beverage available—water.

The official, however, was reluctant to put Daniel on that kind of regimen (vs. 10). He was afraid that it would have adverse effects upon the Hebrews. But Daniel persisted and was eventually given permission to eat his preferred diet for a period of ten days (vs. 14). Ten days out of his three-year course was not too much to risk, but even so, the official only reluctantly gave Daniel and his friends permission to do so. The official was responsible for the captives' welfare, and if they suffered from this new diet, he would suffer from Nebuchadnezzar's wrath (vs. 10). Kings of the ancient world were noted for their tendency to punish the messengers who brought bad news.

Could a period of only ten days really make a difference? In modern society's approach to health, there are a number of examples which demonstrate that ten days can indeed make a difference. One special diet plan advertised on American television promises, "Give us a week, and we'll take off the weight!" More intensive was the regimen of Dr. Pritikin, a nutritionist whose severe low-fat diet was aimed at rapid cholesterol and weight reduction as part of a rehabilitation and conditioning program for seriously ill heart patients. To participate in such a program, one had to spend a week at Pritikin's center. It should also be noted that a patient can recover from major surgery and be discharged from a hospital in well under ten days. In fact, the length of hospital stays are getting shorter and shorter. Thus Daniel's request for ten days as a period of test was reasonable, even though he probably would have liked to have had more time.

Once again, it was not just the ordinary force of human circumstances that opened up this possibility to Daniel and his friends. They were not just better nutritionists or exercise physiologists or intellectually superior to the other students enrolled. They were able to obtain the favor of the official and carry out this program because "God had caused the official to show favor and sympathy to Daniel" (vs. 9). Intelligent as he was, Daniel had still another factor operating in his favor, and that factor was the most important—divine favor. In this situation, God was able to use and bless Daniel and his friends because of their faith in Him and His promises.

Likewise, God can use us today in similar situations. This part of the narrative places emphasis upon the fact that God not only wants us to have spiritually alert minds, but He wants us to have healthy bodies as well. The two are directly related. "At the end of the ten days they looked healthier and better nourished than any of the young men who ate the royal food" (vs. 15). Having passed this ten-day test, Daniel and his friends were able to eat the diet they wanted for the rest of their three years in school. Continuing on this diet for that length of time also contributed to their excellent outcome at the end of the course.

The Final Result

At the end of their three-year course, the final graduation examination was an oral one (vss. 19, 20). Indeed, their oral examiner was the most important person of all, more important than any of the professors they had had during their studies. The final oral examiner was none other than the king himself. He wanted to see what they had accomplished during their period of training and to see if they were satisfactorily qualified to take up posts in the Babylonian government. Once again, Daniel and his friends came through with flying colors: "The king talked with them and he found none to equal Daniel, Hananiah, Mishael and Azariah; so they entered the king's service (vs. 19). Using hyperbole, the text describes them as being ten times better than the other wise men in Nebuchadnezzar's kingdom. This does not mean that Daniel got 100 percent on his exam and that the other wise men of Babylon got only 10 percent. It simply means that the Hebrews were clearly more outstanding than the other students in the course and that they were superior even to the professional wise men who had already taken up their posts. A similar sort of literary phenomenon is found in the story of the burning fiery furnace in Daniel 3. Nebuchadnezzar's workmen were told to heat it "seven times hotter" (vs. 19). This does not mean that the furnace went from 500 degrees, for example, to 3,500 degrees. Rather, it means that it was stoked to a much more intensely hot state, regardless of the absolute temperature involved.

What was the real reason Daniel and his friends did so well on their oral examination before the king? Was it because they had higher IQs? Was it because they were on a healthier program? These things may have helped, but more than these things, it was the direct blessing of God. "To these four young men God gave knowledge and understanding" (vs. 17). Without the blessing of God, these young men would not have done as well as they did. God had a plan and a purpose for them, and He wanted to demonstrate that fact before all of the wise men of Babylon, before their fellow students, and before the king. God has a plan and a blessing for your life, too, although it may not work out just exactly the way it did for these captive students in Babylon.

Dates

We conclude our examination of chapter 1 with a technical note about three minor chronological details related to this chapter. The first has to do with the date in the first verse of the chapter. It says that Nebuchadnezzar came up and besieged Jerusalem in the *third* year of Jehoiakim, king of Judah. Some have criticized this date as inaccurate, claiming that the siege actually took place in Jehoiakim's *fourth* year. This objection is dealt with more fully in chapter 1 of this volume (see page 39). It is sufficient here to point out that if one interprets this date according to the principle of accession year reckoning and the Jewish (fall-to-fall) calendar, the date works out correctly as historically accurate.

The second chronological problem involved here focuses upon the length of time Daniel and his friends studied—three years according to 1:5—and the date upon which the events of chapter 2 took place "in the second year of [Nebuchadnezzar's] reign" (vs. 1). These statements can be harmonized readily when it is realized that 1:5 does not necessarily mean three full years of twelve months each. The first and last years of this study sequence probably were only partial years, just as the academic school year in North America today is more like nine months than twelve.

This explanation involves what is known as "inclusive reckoning," which deals with the way the ancient Hebrews reckoned fractions. For modern readers, 50 percent is the dividing line; anything above that is rounded to the next whole number, and anything below it is deleted. That was not the way the ancient Hebrews did it. For them, any fraction became "inclusive" to the next number. Thus Jesus could be in the tomb for three days even though those three days included only a portion of Friday afternoon, all day Saturday, and a portion of early Sunday morning. According to "inclusive reckoning," that is still three days. Another biblical example of this can be found in 2 Kings 18:9-11 where the siege of Samaria began in the fourth year of Hezekiah and ended in his sixth year, which was "at the end of three years" (2 Kings 18:10). Thus Daniel's three years of schooling may not have been three full years of twelve months each.

The final minor chronological problem in chapter 1 is found in its last verse which says, "Daniel remained there until the first year of King Cyrus" (vs. 21). Since this is the King Cyrus of Persia with whom the book ends (10:1), this is a reference to the entire ministry and lifetime of Daniel in Babylon. But it is put at the end of the very first story of the book which deals with Daniel's arrival in Babylon and his first experiences there.

Obviously, this mention of Cyrus comes from a time seventy years

later, in approximately 536 B.C. It was put here in chapter 1 editori-
ally to anticipate what follows in the book. It is not intended to be a
dateline as is the time statement in verse 1. Rather, it sets the perspective for all of what follows. Some of Daniel's narratives may have
been written earlier and some of them may have been written later,
but the last of them and any editorial comments such as this clearly
came from the Persian period when the book was finished.

■ Applying the Word

Daniel 1

1. Do I have the kind of trust and confidence in God that Daniel
   and his friends did? What kind of an example do they set for
   me? What specific things can I do in my daily life that will
   prepare me to maintain confidence in God when difficult
   situations arise?
2. What troubles or difficult situations have I had to face in my
   life? Have any of them been as severe as what Daniel and his
   friends experienced when they were dragged off as captives
   to Babylon? What kind of attitude do I exhibit when trials
   come into my life?
3. Three of the major events occurring in this chapter resulted
   from something that God "gave." Do I see the same type of
   action by God in my life? What are the gifts He has given to
   me? Is it possible for God to "give" both good things and
   bad? How should I understand the latter?
4. Do I take as good care of my body as did Daniel and his
   friends during their initial experience in Babylon? If I had
   been there with them, would I have requested a special diet?
   Or would I have just eaten what everybody else was eating?
5. How has God given me wisdom and understanding? In what
   areas? With what results? As a student of God's Word, and
   as a student of many other things in life—either in formal or
   informal education—do I sense God giving me insight and
   knowledge as I study? How can I give more of my thinking

and study habits over to God for His blessing?

6. How can I better discern the divine hand behind the apparent jumble of seemingly disorganized world events? Is it possible to see God's intended purpose in the affairs of nations? How? Or do we simply have to trust that He has a plan? How does Daniel 1 (and the rest of the book of Daniel) help me answer this question? In what specific ways have I seen God leading through the events of my life?

■ Researching the Word

1. The fall of Jerusalem and the subsequent Babylonian captivity that so affected Daniel's life are treated in the final chapters of 2 Kings, 2 Chronicles, and Jeremiah. Compare these three accounts. What differences and similarities do you note? Summarize your findings in your Daniel notebook. Ezekiel, along with Jeremiah, was a contemporary with Daniel. Ezekiel's book also tells us much about the captivity. Read the first sixteen chapters of his book. How do these chapters help you fill in your knowledge of what was happening among the Jewish captives in Babylon?

2. In the book of Daniel, Babylon becomes the oppressor of God's people. In the last half of Revelation, Babylon again shows up (this time symbolically) as the oppressor of God's people. Using a concordance, or by reading Revelation, chapters 14–18, find every reference to symbolic Babylon in the book of Revelation. In your Daniel notebook, list the characteristics of symbolic Babylon. Why do you think John chose Babylon as a symbol rather than some other figurative representation?

■ Further Study of the Word

1. For information on what Babylon was like in the time of Daniel, see chapters 4 through 7 in S. H. Horn, *The Spade Confirms the Book.*

2. For information on the training and work of Babylonian scribes, see E. Chiera, *They Wrote on Clay*.

3. For technical topics treated in Babylonian schools and the Babylonian approach to them, see O. Neugebauer, *The Exact Sciences in Antiquity*.

4. Two good general histories of Mesopotamia that include sections on the Neo-Babylonian Empire are H. W. F. Saggs, *The Greatness That Was Babylon* and G. Roux, *Ancient Iraq*.

CHAPTER THREE

Fallen Kings

Daniel 4, 5

Chapters 4 and 5 of Daniel deal with the fate of two kings of the Neo-Babylonian Empire—Nebuchadnezzar, the founder and first great king of that empire (chap. 4), and Belshazzar, the last king of that empire who was not nearly so great (chap. 5). The fact that Daniel's life could encompass the entire history of the Neo-Babylonian Empire shows how short its existence really was. Daniel came to Babylon as a teenager early in Nebuchadnezzar's reign, and he was still there as an old man when Belshazzar died in the palace the night the Persians conquered the city.

Daniel not only lived in Babylon during this long time period, he also interacted on a professional level with both these kings. God used Daniel to bring prophecies to them—prophecies about their kingdom and prophecies about themselves. Thus these two chapters deal not only with these Babylonian kings, but also with Daniel and how he served them. Daniel's role for both kings was similar; he served as an inspired wise man who brought them messages from the true God about their life and times.

Nebuchadnezzar received a message from God through a dream; God spoke to Belshazzar through the writing of a disembodied hand upon the wall of the audience hall of the palace. In both cases the kings needed somebody to interpret God's message, and in both cases the wise men of Babylon were inadequate for the task. Daniel had to be called because the mysterious messages came from the true God whom he served. Both messages were messages of judgments that would fall upon the kings. They were both to be judged according to the contents of the prophecies which Daniel interpreted for them. And in both cases all happened just as Daniel predicted.

However, there is a significant difference between the fate of these two kings. Nebuchadnezzar received a prolonged sentence of insanity, but he eventually came back from it, repented, and turned in faith toward the true God. Belshazzar, on the other hand, received his judgment on the very night the prophecy came to him. With his death that night, the Neo-Babylonian Empire passed into Medo-Persian hands.

The themes of these two chapters are similar, then, even though they are developed in different ways. This thematic link binds these two chapters together at the center of the chiastic literary structure of the Aramaic section of the book (chaps. 2–7). In this structure chapter 2 is linked thematically with chapter 7; chapter 3 is linked thematically with chapter 6. And at the center of this ladder, chapter 4 is linked with chapter 5. Thus, chapters 4 and 5 stand as a linked pair at the center of this chiastic structure. They are linked together by the nature of their contents, and they have been placed side by side to further emphasize that connection. (For a further discussion of the chiastic literary structure of the historical section of Daniel, see chapter 1, pages 44-47).

■ Getting Into the Word

Daniel 4

Read through Daniel 4 twice. During the second reading, complete the following exercises in your Daniel notebook.

1. List the sin or sins of which Nebuchadnezzar is guilty in this chapter.
2. What specific indications can you find that show that Nebuchadnezzar had an opportunity to repent? What indications are there regarding the amount of time given him for repentance? What means did God use to try to bring him to repentance? Would you say that this chapter reveals God as long-suffering and merciful—or arbitrary, vengeful, and judgmental? Give reasons for your answer.
3. Divide a page in your Daniel notebook into two columns. In the first column, list the symbols God used to speak to

Nebuchadnezzar in his dream. In the second column, list Daniel's interpretation of each symbol.

4. What is the principal unit of time used in the prophecy to Nebuchadnezzar? Compare Daniel 7:25 and 12:7, where this same unit is used. What do you think the prophecy means by the term "times"? Give a reason for your answer.

5. Was it fair for God to use insanity as a judgment upon Nebuchadnezzar? What indications can you find in Daniel 4 as to whether Nebuchadnezzar thought the judgment was fair?

6. Compare Nebuchadnezzar's reaction to Daniel's message at the beginning of chapter 4 and at its end. Write a paragraph or two about the lessons to be learned from those reactions.

■ Exploring the Word

The Dream of the Great Tree

The story in chapter 4 is cast mainly as a first-person report from Nebuchadnezzar himself. He begins the account in this way:

> King Nebuchadnezzar, To the peoples, nations and men of every language, who live in all the world: May you prosper greatly! It is my pleasure to tell you about the miraculous signs and wonders that the Most High God has performed for me (4:1, 2).

After a brief poetic passage in which the king praises this great God for His majesty and dominion, he goes on to relate his experience. Nebuchadnezzar's expressions of praise are a good lesson for us. We, too, should praise God for the great things He has done for us. This is one of the lessons of chapter 4. Just as God worked on Nebuchadnezzar's behalf in ancient times, so He can work for us today. Perhaps the way He works for us will not take the same form as His actions in Nebuchadnezzar's behalf, but the narrative in this chapter assures us that God is powerful and that He intervenes in the affairs of life for the benefit of His children. When He does, and we see His hand at work, we should praise Him as Nebuchadnezzar did.

Nebuchadnezzar did not date this account of God's dealings with him, but we have some indication of the time frame in which these events occurred. The king reports that he was in his palace, contented and prosperous. Such a description would apply most naturally to a period sometime during the middle of his forty-three-year reign. During the first third of his reign, Nebuchadnezzar took the army out on almost constant campaigns. During the last third, he went back on the road with the army again. Thus, it was especially during the middle third of his long reign that he was at peace and prosperous, because his major military conquests had been accomplished by that time.

One night during this prosperous and peaceful period, the king was asleep in the palace when there came to him a most impressive dream. This was no ordinary dream, and Nebuchadnezzar felt that it was of vital importance to him to find out what it meant. In the case of his earlier dream described in Daniel 2, Nebuchadnezzar could not remember the content when he awoke; this time, he remembered his dream clearly. So he called his wise men and diviners, recounted the dream to them, and demanded an interpretation. No one could explain it to him (vss. 7, 8).

Finally, Daniel was called. The junior wise men could not accomplish the task, so their chief was called. Note that at first Nebuchadnezzar refers to Daniel by his Babylonian name of Belteshazzar. The king told Daniel that in his dream he had seen a great tree. The tree was enormous and strong and visible to the ends of the earth. It also provided shade for the animals that lived under it and fruit for the birds who lived in its branches (vss. 10-12).

The second scene of the king's dream, however, was not so pleasant. A holy messenger angel came down from heaven with a decree that the tree be cut down, including branches, leaves, and fruit; the birds and animals that had previously lived in its protection were to be scattered. But all was not lost, for the stump of the tree was to be bound after the tree was cut down, and it would remain in the ground (vss. 13-15).

At this point in the dream, the angel made a transition in his instruction and explanation, moving from the symbol of the tree to the actuality of what the tree represented. The tree clearly represented a man and his fate. The angel indicated that the man so represented would live among the animals and plants of the field, just like the stump of this tree. This man's mind would be changed into the mind of an animal, just like those he was to live among. All of this would last until seven "times," or years, would pass over him (vss. 16, 17). Presumably, the judgment would then be lifted, although the angel did not directly prophesy the man's actual restoration at the end of the seven years.

If you had been one of the wise men summoned by the king to explain this dream, what would it have meant to you? Remember, you would not have the clear hindsight we have today in reading the entire story.

It would have been clear that the dream applied to a man, for the words of the angel made that plain. But what man? It seems obvious to us, as we read the story today, that Nebuchadnezzar was the man involved. But would this have been the natural explanation to occur to the wise men facing the task of interpreting the dream? Probably not. More likely, they would have immediately thought in terms of an enemy of Nebuchadnezzar. Because of the fate of the man in the dream, their first inclination would probably have been to pick out the king or opponent who was giving Nebuchadnezzar the most trouble and apply the dream to him.

If you had been one of the wise men commanded to interpret the dream, the one thing you would *not* want to do would be to apply the dream to Nebuchadnezzar! After all, messengers who brought bad news to the king could easily suffer his wrath. However, the wise men probably would not have thought of this interpretation anyway. It simply would not have occurred to them that a king so rich and powerful and famous could suffer such an affliction. At the time, mental illness was thought to be the work of demons, and how could demons afflict a man so obviously blessed by the gods?

Thus Daniel's interpretation ran contrary not only to what the wise men thought about Nebuchadnezzar, but to the very theology of their belief system. A man so blessed by the gods could not be cursed by them at the same time too! If things had been going badly for Nebuchadnezzar, it could indicate that the gods were angry with him. If so, such an application of the dream might be true. But not now in a time of prosperity and peace.

Daniel's Interpretation

When Daniel received the interpretation of this dream from the true God, he, too, was shocked (vs. 19). Like the other wise men, Daniel was astounded that such a fate could happen to so prominent and powerful a figure. In chapter 1 Daniel had written that God had given Jehoiakim of Judah into Nebuchadnezzar's hand (vs. 2). And if God had given Nebuchadnezzar control of the king of His own covenant people, how much more true must that be of those kings and kingdoms elsewhere in the world that Nebuchadnezzar had conquered? In his prayer of thanksgiving for the gift of the dream and its interpretation in chapter 2, Daniel had praised God because He "sets up kings and deposes them" (vs. 21). Given the prominence to which Nebuchadnezzar had come, it certainly looked as though God was the One who had placed him in his lofty position. Clearly, God had exalted Nebuchadnezzar and given him great power. But now He was going to demonstrate the other side of the coin. Whom He had set up, He could also depose, and Nebuchadnezzar was about to be deposed. That was what shocked and surprised Daniel about the interpretation of the dream in chapter 4. But in spite of his surprise, he went ahead and told the king what the dream meant.

Like Nathan before David, Daniel reluctantly carried out his assignment. With tact he pointed out that the dream applied to Nebuchadnezzar. But he couched the prophetic word with concern for the king, "My lord, if only the dream applied to your enemies and its meaning to your adversaries!" (vs. 19). Before God gave him the interpretation, Daniel probably thought the dream *did* apply to Nebuchadnezzar's enemies. Certainly, that is what the other wise men would have thought. Once God spoke to him, however, Daniel could do nothing but clarify and present God's message for the king.

After describing the great tree, Daniel said, "You, O king, are that tree!" (vs. 22). This part of the message was not so difficult, for he could go on to praise the strength and greatness of the tree-king. Then came the harder part found in the second act of the dream:

> You will be driven away from people and will live with the wild animals; you will eat grass like cattle and be drenched with the dew of heaven. Seven times will pass by for you until you acknowledge that the Most High is sovereign over the kingdoms of men and gives them to anyone he wishes (vs. 25).

Daniel did not end his prophetic sermon without offering hope. The prophecy included restoration as its final element. Daniel concluded with an appeal to the king, calling him to repentance:

> Therefore, O king, be pleased to accept my advice: Renounce your sins by doing what is right, and your wickedness by being kind to the oppressed. It may be that then your prosperity will continue (vs. 27).

Daniel did not appeal for the king to repent merely with words; he called for actions that were commensurate with the depth and sincerity of his repentance. He called for right deeds and restoration. In the name of the oppressed, Daniel challenged this fearful conqueror who had wrought so much destruction across the Near East. Nebuchadnezzar had oppressed others to the limit; now he had the opportunity to redress those wrongs and make them right. He had the power to do so. The question was, Would he do so?

The dream and the prophet's appeal pointed the king to repentance, confession, and restoration. Nebuchadnezzar's military exploits were noteworthy; could he also leave behind him a record of restoration after those conquests? It would take a great man and a humble man to do so. But if Nebuchadnezzar were not humble enough to do so himself, God would do the humbling for him.

The Results

The kings of Judah would not repent of their folly, which led to the downfall of their kingdom and the exile of their people. Could we really expect a pagan king such as Nebuchadnezzar to repent in response to the prophet's appeal? Think about what would be involved in such a repentance.

The king would be admitting that he should not have made the conquests he had carried out. That the oppression he had imposed upon the various countries of the ancient Near East should not have been imposed. That he should not have imprisoned the war captives. That exiles, such as the very prophet who stood before him, should not have been brought to Babylon and that they should be returned to their own lands. In essence, the king would be saying that a large part of what he had done as king—some of his greatest exploits—were wrong. It would have taken a great and humble man to admit this, and Nebuchadnezzar was not up to—or down to—the task. He would not bow in repentance.

Although the king refused to submit to God when He appealed to him through Daniel and the interpretation of the dream, God gave Nebuchadnezzar more time to think it over. He gave him plenty of time. He gave him a whole year. Still Nebuchadnezzar would not yield and repent. One year later, he was walking on the roof of his palace. Perhaps he was thinking about the impressive dream he had had a year earlier (vs. 29). His response—a stubborn rejection of the prophet's appeal—was unchanged.

The form in which he expressed his refusal is interesting. It was couched in a statement of boastful pride: "Is not this the great Babylon I have built as the royal residence, by my mighty power and for the glory of my majesty?" (vs. 30).

Was there any basis in fact for this boasting? Yes, quite a bit. Nebuchadnezzar had enlarged and beautified Babylon on a grand scale. Prior to his time, the city had consisted mainly of a smaller area—"the inner city" or central portion. Nebuchadnezzar added a new line of outer walls. This had the effect of strengthening the city's defenses and enlarging its area at the same time. Inside these outer walls, he built a new palace. He also built the western section of the city across the Euphrates River. (See map of Babylon on page 79.) We know he was responsible for much of this construction because thousands upon thousands of the broken clay bricks which survive in the ruins of ancient Babylon have Nebuchadnezzar's name stamped upon them.

In addition to physically building up the city of Babylon, Nebuchadnezzar also built the nation into an empire by his political and military conquests. His father, Nabopolassar, threw off the Assyrian yoke, freeing Babylonian forces to undertake more wide-ranging campaigns. But it was his son, Nebuchadnezzar, who welded the conquests made in those campaigns into an empire.

Then, too, there is the matter of the length of Nebuchadnezzar's reign. The foundation of the Neo-Babylonian Empire can be dated to 605 B.C., the year Nebuchadnezzar came to the throne. The demise of this empire can be fixed in 539 B.C., the year the Medo-Persian army conquered Babylon. Since Nebuchadnezzar reigned for forty-three years, his rulership spanned some two-thirds of the entire time the Neo-Babylonian Empire existed.

So Nebuchadnezzar had solid reasons for glorying in his achievements in terms of building the city of Babylon, building an empire, and ruling over it for much of the time it existed. There is, however, another side to his accomplishments, a darker side. If Assyrian practices are any example, much of the construction of the city of Babylon was carried out by slave laborers captured in various military campaigns. The extension of Nebuchadnezzar's empire exacted a high cost in human lives—both of the defeated and of his own soldiers who died in battle.

It used to be thought that Nebuchadnezzar's reign was one long, uninterrupted rule. But now that we possess his annals for the first eleven years of his reign, we know that in his tenth year there was a revolt against him in Babylon. This revolt was so serious that even in the palace there was hand-to-hand fighting in which the king himself was involved! Nebuchadnezzar's achievements may have been impressive, but they came with a high price tag for many of his subjects—some of whom were not entirely peaceful and accepting of his rule.

In spite of the suffering his projects had cost, Nebuchadnezzar could still boast about his own greatness and the greatness of his accomplishments. But the heavenly watchers recorded his boasting and pride. The whole picture of what these accomplishments had cost in terms of human suffering was open before God, and He did not approve. Nebuchadnezzar was raising himself up to an almost quasi-divine status, like the figure of the king of Babylon who represents the devil in Isaiah 14:12-15.

Now Nebuchadnezzar was to receive his deserved punishment predicted in the prophetic dream of a year earlier. Now he would be cast down to the ground and take his position with the lowliest of the low, with the animals themselves. He had had a full year of probation in which to repent of what he had done and his pride in it, but he made no such move toward the true God. Now it was time for his sentence to be carried out.

The type of insanity to which Nebuchadnezzar was subjected is uncommon, but not unknown in modern psychiatric practice. The technical name for animal-like, or more specifically "wolflike," behavior by human beings is *lycanthropy*.

In view of the general situation that would exist in the case of a king who was incapacitated in this way for such a long period of time, the question arises: How did Nebuchadnezzar manage to hold on to his throne in spite of his madness? This would have been an ideal time for a usurper to assassinate the insane king and take the throne in his place.

The probable reason this did not happen has to do with the ancients' view of mental illness. They believed it was caused by demons, minor gods who were malevolent toward human beings. They also believed that if a person was deliberately killed while suffering from insanity, the demon-god who had caused the mental illness would cause it to come upon the murderer. Thus no one would risk acquiring mental illness by killing a person so afflicted. Babylonian theology, or psychology, probably protected Nebuchadnezzar during the time of his incapacitation.

Several times the text gives the length of time the madness was to last as "seven times" (vss. 16, 23, 25). By a process of elimination, it

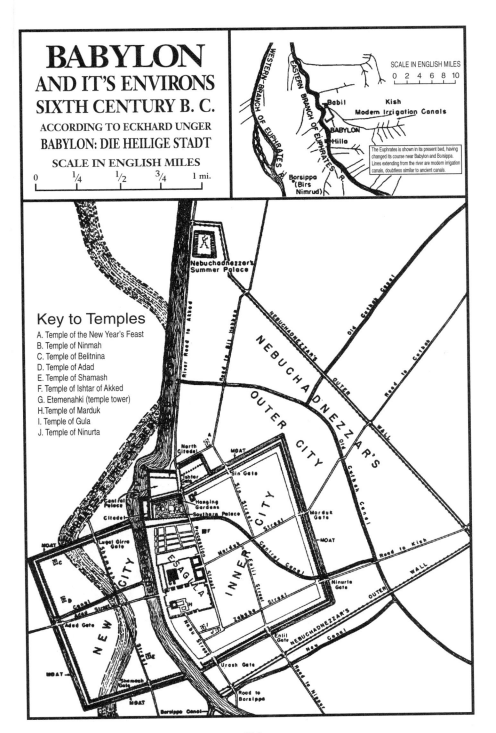

BABYLON
AND IT'S ENVIRONS
SIXTH CENTURY B. C.
ACCORDING TO ECKHARD UNGER
BABYLON: DIE HEILIGE STADT
SCALE IN ENGLISH MILES

0   1/4   1/2   3/4   1 mi.

SCALE IN ENGLISH MILES
0 2 4 6 8 10

Babil
Kish
Modern Irrigation Canals

BABYLON
Hilla

Borsippa
(Birs Nimrud)

The Euphrates is shown in its present bed, having changed its course near Babylon and Borsippa. Lines extending from the river are modern irrigation canals, doubtless similar to ancient canals.

WESTERN BRANCH OF EUPHRATES R.
EASTERN BRANCH OF EUPHRATES R.

Nebuchadnezzar's Summer Palace

Key to Temples
A. Temple of the New Year's Feast
B. Temple of Ninmah
C. Temple of Belitnina
D. Temple of Adad
E. Temple of Shamash
F. Temple of Ishtar of Akked
G. Etemenahki (temple tower)
H. Temple of Marduk
I. Temple of Gula
J. Temple of Ninurta

NEBUCHADNEZZAR'S OUTER CITY

Old Cobar Canal
Road to Cobar

River Road to Akked
Road to Ali Hobba

North Citadel
Ishtar Gate
Sin Gate
Central Palace
Hanging Gardens
Southern Palace
Citadel
Legal Girra Gate
Procession Street
Sin Street
Marduk Gate
Marduk Street
Enlil Street
ESAGILA
Central Canal
INNER CITY
Nebu Street
Zababa Street
Ninurta Gate
Enlil Gate
Urash Gate
Adad Gate
Shamash Gate

NEW CITY
Adad Street
Adad Canal

NEBUCHADNEZZAR'S New Canal
Road to Kish
Road to Nippur
Road to Borsippa
Borsippo Canal

MOAT
WALL
OUTER

can be seen that "years" is the only time unit with which the word "times" fits in this chapter. So it has been understood since pre-Christian times. The Greek Old Testament of Daniel, chapter 4, translates this word as "years." Thus in Nebuchadnezzar's dream, "times" means "years." The king was to be incapacitated and insane for seven years.

We may consider the judgment severe, but it had the desired effect. At the end of the time, when Nebuchadnezzar came back to his normal senses, he also came back to a recognition and knowledge of the true God (compare 2:47; 3:28, 29). He acknowledged God in his psalm of praise at the beginning of the chapter (vss. 2, 3) and also in his song of praise at the end of the chapter (vss. 34, 35). Notice that he glorified and praised the God of heaven *first* before he told about the return of his kingdom and his restoration to his position and power (vs. 34). He now saw divine and human affairs in their correct priority. In this entire recital, Nebuchadnezzar's closing statement was: "Those [like me] who walk in pride he [the Most High God] is able to humble" (vs. 37).

One of the questions we asked at the beginning of this chapter was this: Was God fair to judge Nebuchadnezzar in this way? And now we can see that the ultimate answer to that questions is Yes. It *was* fair of God. Even Nebuchadnezzar himself acknowledged that fact at the end of the story. While he was out with the animals, he probably was not able to see the great central fact of God in his experience. But when he was restored to his right mind and looked back over the entire affair, he could see God's hand in it all. At this juncture in his life, he became a believer in the true God, in contrast with the false gods of polytheism he had worshiped previously.

Daniel, the prophet of God, was on the scene of action to explain to the king what all of this meant. And God continued to speak to Nebuchadnezzar. As severe as God's judgment on Nebuchadnezzar may appear, ultimately this experience brought about his conversion to the true God. So it is not surprising that after chapter 4 we hear nothing more about Nebuchadnezzar in the book of Daniel. There is a spiritual pilgrimage in the book that tells of Daniel's own experience, and there is also the story of Nebuchadnezzar's spiritual pilgrimage. He traveled the road from being the most powerful king of his time—a proud, egotistical ruler—to the point where he became a humble, trusting, and praising believer in the true God. At the close of chapter 4, we leave Nebuchadnezzar rejoicing in the salvation that had come to his royal house that day.

Nebuchadnezzar's Lesson Is for Us

Although we don't have the personal power and authority Nebuchadnezzar wielded as ruler of Babylon, we still can learn from his experience. Like him, we probably tend to think better of ourselves than we should. Like him, we praise our own achievements, large or small. "Is this not great Babylon which I have built" still echoes in our experience today. This kind of pride and self-congratulation did not die with the death of the Neo-Babylonian Empire. It lives on today in human nature and continues to manifest itself in various ways. It is the foundation of the modern religion of humanism, which holds that human beings are so competent mentally and physically that we do not need help from any outside source such as God. But just when we get to this point in our experience, something comes along to disturb that self-confidence and to throw us back into the arms of our heavenly Father who alone can meet our ultimate needs. The problem can be individual—a health crisis. Or it can be family related—the death of a loved one. It can be something local—a flood or fire. Or national and international—war or famine. Whatever form the crisis may take, we learn that our own devices are not adequate to cope. Our dependence cannot be on self; it must lie in something greater than our own abilities. Like Nebuchadnezzar, we must ultimately find our reason for living in something greater than, and outside of, ourselves. The philosophy of humanism and our human pride are ultimately bankrupt when it comes to the deepest needs of our beings. We find our highest position in life when we kneel humbly at the foot of the cross. Nebuchadnezzar found that out, and our experience leads us to the same conclusion.

We sometimes complain about these testing situations. "Why me?"

is a constant cry when trouble comes. The reverses we experience in life may not be as direct or as severe as those that Nebuchadnezzar faced, but they should have the same end result. We should be able to see the hand of God leading us through those trying experiences; we should ultimately be able to see how He has used them to refine our characters and teach us to rely on Him in trying times. At the end of his experience, Nebuchadnezzar voiced no complaint against God for the insanity which had fallen upon him. It was not too severe. It did not last too long. There was no argument with God; Nebuchadnezzar simply stood back and praised Him for the part that He had taken in his life.

We, too, should be able to look back on our past experiences and see the way God has led us. Properly understood, we would not change anything the leadership of God allows to come into our lives, even though some episodes may have been hard and painful at the time. When we come to the final point that Nebuchadnezzar did, the hardness of those experiences fades away and is swallowed up in praise to the God who has led us, even through the valley of the shadow.

■ Getting Into the Word

Daniel 5

Read Daniel 5 two times. Then complete the following exercises, thinking through the issues in this chapter and using your Daniel notebook.

1. List the sins of Belshazzar brought to light in Daniel 5. Is any single sin more central to the story and/or more serious than the others? If so, why?
2. Was Daniel present when the people assembled for the banquet described in chapter 5? What reason can you suggest for his presence or absence?
3. On what did Daniel base his remarks to Belshazzar when he began their conversation? To what experience did he point?

Is there a lesson for us in this? If so, what is it?

4. List the specific elements of the judgment that was to come upon Belshazzar according to Daniel's interpretation of the handwriting on the wall. Even at this late date, did Belshazzar have an opportunity to repent? If so, when? Could he have avoided this judgment? If not, why not?

5. In chapter 4, Nebuchadnezzar received a judgment from God, but he came back from it to return to his rulership of the kingdom. In chapter 5, Belshazzar received a judgment from God, but he did not recover from it or maintain his throne. Was God being arbitrary and unjust in Belshazzar's case? What evidence can you supply for your answer? What was the difference between the two situations?

■ Exploring the Word

The Banquet

Daniel 5 opens with Belshazzar appointing a banquet. This may seem strange when one remembers that at the very time Belshazzar was calling for a banquet, a division of the Persian army was posted outside the walls besieging the city! Was not this a foolish time to be involved in such a celebration?

It might look so at first, but in light of all the defenses behind which this banquet took place, we can better appreciate Belshazzar's self-confidence. Babylon was defended by *two* sets of walls, the outer walls and the inner walls. Both were actually double walls. The two inner walls were twelve and twenty-two feet thick respectively. The two walls making up the outer defenses were twenty-four and twenty-six feet thick. Thus any enemy who wanted to get into the inner city, where the palace and main temple were located, had almost eighty-five feet of walls to get through or over, and these came in four different sections, all of them defended (see map of the city on page 79). No wonder Belshazzar felt secure enough to hold a banquet in spite of the besieging army outside the city!

The invitees to this banquet included the upper class of official

Babylonian society—a thousand of the lords or nobles of the realm. The king also invited his wife, his secondary wives, the concubines from the royal harem (vss. 1, 3), and possibly his mother—the "queen" of verse 10, although this could be a reference to Belshazzar's main wife.

The banquet involved a lot of drinking, both wine and probably beer (vs. 2). The Babylonians were famous for their beer making, and some of the tablets describing their procedure for making beer have been found. Beer is probably what the Bible calls "strong drink" and which it condemns more strongly than it condemns fermented wine. Modern statistics for crimes and auto accidents demonstrate that alcohol is involved in a large percentage of such situations—with disastrous results. Alcohol is a drug that affects the faculties of judgment in the human mind and its higher, moral thought patterns. Belshazzar was no exception to this effect.

The king went beyond merely having a banquet at which quite a bit of drinking was done. He brought out the vessels that had been taken from the temple of Yahweh, or Jehovah, in Jerusalem and used them as receptacles from which to drink alcohol (vs. 3; see also 2 Kings 24:12, 13). Belshazzar may have also used vessels from the temples of other Near Eastern gods. Clearly, the use to which he put these vessels indicated his contempt for God, from whose temple they had come.

Belshazzar's drinking from the temple vessels also involved certain theological beliefs. According to Babylonian theology, many gods existed in heaven. These gods acted on earth through their representatives so that when a particular event took place on earth, it meant that the same action had also taken place in the realm of the gods. For example, when Babylon scored a victory over one of its enemies, this indicated that in the heavens, Marduk, the god of Babylon, had defeated the god of that country. Thus earthly events reflected what had happened as well among the gods. So for Belshazzar to drink from the vessels that had come from Yahweh's temple was an expression, for him, of the superiority of his god over that of the Jews. Unfortunately for Belshazzar, his theology was false; he was actually engaged in an act of blasphemy against the true God.

The Handwriting on the Wall

God's response to this act of blasphemy by Belshazzar and his nobles was sent in the form of a prophecy written upon the wall of the throne room or audience chamber in which the banquet was held (vss. 5, 6). Thanks to the spade of the archaeologist, we have a pretty good idea where this occurred. The palace area of Babylon was located just inside the great Ishtar gate on the north side of the inner city (see the map of Babylon and its environs on page 79). Coming south through the processional way, a traveler would pass through that gate and turn right toward the Euphrates to enter the palace area. The buildings of the palace were arranged around a central courtyard; the building on the south side was the one in which the king held audiences, and so it probably was the building in which Belshazzar held his banquet.

The outside of this building was covered with ornate and elaborate figures framed in colored enameled bricks. Among the figures portrayed were lions reminiscent of the first "beast" of Daniel 7:4, which symbolized Babylon. The walls inside the building, however, were plain white, so in whatever medium the disembodied hand wrote, the letters would have stood out distinctly against that background.

Belshazzar, and no doubt his nobles as well, were shocked when the writing appeared on the wall. In his fright, his "legs gave way," and he "turned pale" (vs. 6). Everyone in the room was astounded. Naturally, everyone wondered what the strange writing meant. An immediate search began for someone who could read the mysterious writing. The wise men of Babylon came, but they could not offer an answer (vss. 7-9).

Then the queen (vs. 10), probably the queen mother of Belshazzar, remembered the old days, half a century earlier, when Daniel had served at the court as a wise man, superior to all of the other wise men of Babylon. On at least two occasions, Daniel had been able to unlock the mysteries of Nebuchadnezzar's dreams, and this stuck in the memory of the queen mother. At her urging, Daniel was summoned (vss. 10-13).

The interview that ensued between Daniel and Belshazzar covered three main points. One, of course, was the interpretation of the writing on the wall. As a preface, however, Belshazzar made an offer to anyone who could interpret the writing. He proposed to make that person the third ruler in the kingdom and to give him the emblems and tokens of that office (vs. 16).

Why would Belshazzar offer to make the successful person the "third" ruler in the kingdom? It would be much more natural to offer to make him the "second" ruler. Or failing that, to simply give him great honor. But an offer of the "third" position in the kingdom seems oddly specific. Why the "third" position?

It all becomes clear when we understand the political situation in Babylon at the time. The kingship of Babylon was involved in an unusual arrangement just then. The official king was Nabonidus, Belshazzar's father. But because of his extended absence from the kingdom, he had made Belshazzar co-regent. In his own words, he "entrusted the kingship to him [Belshazzar]." For ten years while Nabonidus was away in Tema of Arabia, Belshazzar had remained in Babylon and administered the kingdom.

Now, however, Nabonidus had returned. But the situation had become even more threatening than it had been when he was off in Arabia. With the Medes and Persians assaulting the eastern frontier of the empire, Babylon was in danger of crumbling. Two rulers were vitally necessary at this time—one in the field to meet the onslaught of the enemy, and the other in the capital to hold the kingdom securely in his control. Nabonidus took the role of field commander and led one division of the Babylonian army out to the Tigris River to meet Cyrus and his troops. Belshazzar stayed in the city with another division of the army to protect the capital. Nabonidus was defeated on the fourteenth day of Tishri, and the city of Babylon fell to the Persian army two days later. Through the use of tables compiled by modern astronomers and Assyriologists, the day that Babylon fell can be identified as October 12, 539 B.C. in terms of our calendar.

This explains Belshazzar's offer of the "third" position in the kingdom to anyone who could interpret the writing on the wall.

Nabonidus occupied the first position as senior king. As co-king, Belshazzar was the second in the kingdom, and the successful interpreter would be elevated to the third highest position, that of prime minister, serving under these two kings.

Later historians lost the knowledge of this situation in Babylon and even of Belshazzar's existence. Only an inhabitant of Babylon in the sixth century B.C. could have known of such an unusual arrangement and used such a specific, yet irregular, designation as "*third* highest ruler in the kingdom" (vs. 16, emphasis supplied). Daniel received that honor because he interpreted the writing (vs. 29), but he occupied the post only a few hours. Then the Persian army conquered the city, and Belshazzar was killed (vs. 30).

The last part of the interview between Daniel and Belshazzar involved Belshazzar's knowledge of recent Babylonian history. Daniel referred Belshazzar to the case of Nebuchadnezzar and the results of his pride as outlined in chapter 4. Not only did Daniel recall this experience to Belshazzar, he fearlessly declared that he ought to have paid attention to it. It should have been an instructive example to Belshazzar, but he did not humble himself (vss. 18-21).

If Belshazzar had taken Nebuchadnezzar's experience into account, he would never have committed the sacrilege of drinking from the vessels from Yahweh's temple. Nebuchadnezzar's experience should have taught him to respect the true God whose might and power could humble the greatest ruler of the kingdom. But he chose to ignore this warning. "You . . . have not humbled yourself, though you knew all this," Daniel accused the king (vs. 22). Belshazzar was sinning against light and knowledge; he was not in darkness and ignorance concerning the true God (vss. 22-24).

As a matter of fact, Belshazzar and his father, Nabonidus, had deliberately chosen other gods to worship. They worshiped not only Marduk, the regular and prominent god of Babylon, but Sin, the moon god as well. Nabonidus was a special devotee of this god. He selected temples of the moon god to rebuild and refurbish, in Syria as well as in Babylonia. He even built a temple to Sin in Arabia.

It is interesting to see this connection with the moon god in the light of events as they occurred in Babylon that October night the city was taken. The final Persian assault on Babylon began on the night of the fifteenth of Tishri and was completed by the morning of the sixteenth (the Babylonian day extended from sundown to sundown). On the night of the fifteenth of a lunar month such as Tishri, a full moon would be shining. Thus Babylon fell when Sin, the moon god, was at his fullest and most powerful. Although elevated by Nabonidus to a position of prominence in the Babylonian pantheon, the moon god had no power against the decree of Yahweh, the true God, who had predicted the overthrow of Babylon by the Medes and Persians. God's power was shown to be sovereign over all of the elements of nature and man. Nothing could turn Him aside from the accomplishment of His purposes—certainly not the power (weakness!) of the false god of the moon.

These events display another interesting detail in terms of the calendar. The month of Tishri was the seventh month of both the Jewish and the Babylonian calendar. The Hebrew festival of Yom Kippur, the Day of Atonement, occurred on the tenth day of Tishri. In other words, the Jewish Day of Atonement occurred just five days before the city of Babylon fell. When Daniel read the writing on the wall, he interpreted the meaning of the third word written there, *tekel*, as signifying, "You have been weighed on the scales and found wanting" (vs. 27). The verb here is in the past tense—"you have been weighed." When might God have made such a judgment concerning Babylon? Of all the days in the Jewish calendar, the Day of Atonement was the day of judgment par excellence. It was a day of judgment in the camp of ancient Israel, and it is still considered to be a day of judgment in modern rituals of the synagogue. There would have been no more appropriate time for God to have passed sentence upon Babylon and Belshazzar than the Day of Atonement, which preceded the overthrow of the kingdom by just five days.

There actually were four words written on the wall (vs. 25). The first two were the same word repeated—*mene*. This word meant, according to Daniel, "God has numbered the days of your reign and brought it to an end" (vs. 26). It is interesting that this word was repeated. This can be meaningful in terms of the two rulers—Nabonidus and Belshazzar—who ruled together on the same throne at the time. One would not outlive the other and reign on; the reign of both was to come to an end at the same time—Belshazzar through death, and Nabonidus through defeat and exile.

We have already looked at the third word written on the wall, *tekel,* and its meaning. *Parsin,* the fourth and final word, told of the power that would receive the kingdom when the Chaldean dynasty fell. *Parsin* referred to the Persians; the Medo-Persian Empire was to expand to incorporate into it what had formerly belonged to Babylon. Or as Daniel interpreted it, "Your kingdom is divided and given to the Medes and Persians" (vs. 28).

The story of how the Medo-Persian army conquered Babylon is told by the Greek historian Herodotus, who visited the region a century after these events took place. The inhabitants told him that the Persians diverted the Euphrates River and then marched into the city through the riverbed, thereby bypassing the intricate system of fortress walls (*The Histories,* I:189-192). All this occurred in Tishri, the month we call October. That is the month in which the Euphrates River is at its lowest ebb. Thus it is not entirely clear just how much water the Persians would have had to divert from the river. At any rate, they gained entrance to the city through the riverbed.

There was still the obstacle of the city gates on the piers beside the river. These were probably only lightly defended, but the Persians would still have had to force them open. The question is, how?

The most prevalent theory is that a traitorous fifth column in the city, made up of Babylonians who were disgusted with the rule of Nabonidus, were willing to open the gates for their conquering deliverers. Nabonidus was an unpopular king, and texts exist, written after the fall of Babylon, which even suggest that he was mad. Of course, this could be Persian propaganda written to insure a ready acceptance among the populace. But one answer to how the Persians were able to breach the city walls along the river is that traitors inside the city willingly opened them.

Another possibility can be suggested from Isaiah 45:1-3 where God promises to go before Cyrus' troops and give Babylon into his hand:

This is what the Lord says to his anointed, to Cyrus, whose right hand I take hold of to subdue nations before him and to strip kings of their armor, to open doors before him so that gates will not be shut: I will go before you and will level the mountains; I will break down the gates of bronze and cut through bars of iron. I will give you the treasures of darkness, riches stored in secret places, so that you may know that I am the Lord, the God of Israel, who summons you by name.

This remarkable prophecy has been a stumbling block to critical interpreters of the Bible. They cannot see how Isaiah, who lived in the eighth century B.C., could prophesy so specifically of these events which did not occur until the sixth century B.C. The prophecy even points out Cyrus by name almost two centuries before he accomplished these deeds. To fit these facts with their understanding of how Scripture was written, some interpreters have hypothesized a "second Isaiah" who lived in the sixth century B.C. and who would have known of these events and Cyrus' name.

To those who believe that Scripture is inspired by God, however, this prophecy is simply an evidence of His remarkable foreknowledge and of how He has chosen to give this knowledge to His servants the prophets. With such evidences of God speaking through His prophets, what faith we should have in God's word through them!

When God prophesies events to take place in human history, He can use a variety of means to bring them about. He can simply foresee what human actors will do on the stage of history. In other instances, He intervenes more directly. We see that intervention clearly in certain places in the book of Daniel, especially in chapters 3 and 6, which we will study in the next chapter of this book.

In chapter 5, the mysterious handwriting that appeared on Belshazzar's wall was a clear example of God's direct, miraculous intervention in human affairs. Everyone present at the feast knew that this writing was supernatural in origin. No Babylonian artist painted those words on the wall; it was either an angel or God Himself. And if God intervened so directly in Belshazzar's palace, then the distinct possibility exists that He, or His angel, acted in a similar way with the latches on the river gates of the city.

Certainly, God sent an angel to miraculously open prison gates to free Peter (Acts 12:10). So perhaps it was not Babylonian traitors who opened the river gates after all; maybe it was the same angel who had written on the palace wall a short time earlier. If one supernatural action occurred in the palace, then surely it isn't difficult to conceive of another supernatural action following soon thereafter a short distance away. Perhaps God did not rely upon a human hand to fulfill His word to Isaiah regarding Cyrus; perhaps He Himself acted to fulfill His own word, just as He said He would.

The Results

The events of this historic night ended with several significant results. Belshazzar was deposed and killed (Daniel 5:30). Although the prophecy of the writing hand had broad, political implications, it was, first of all, a personal prophecy to Belshazzar. To him, the prophecy specifically meant his own individual downfall. "That very night Belshazzar, king of the Babylonians, was slain" (vs. 30) as the Persian troops broke into the undefended palace. The Greek historian Xenophon (*Cyropaedia* VII, V, 24-32) confirms the Bible statement. He doesn't refer to Belshazzar by name, but he relates how there was a banquet taking place in the Babylonian palace that night and how a king of Babylon was killed. He also tells us why that king was killed. On a hunting trip, Nabonidus, chief king of Babylon, had earlier killed the son of Gobryas, the Persian general who was to lead his troops into the city the night Babylon was overthrown. In revenge for the death of his son, Gobryas killed the son of Nabonidus.

But more important than Belshazzar's fate was the fate of nations that occurred that night. The shifting fortunes of history turned away from Babylon to crown Persia as the next great world empire. Medo-Persia was to extend its borders even farther than Babylon had. The city of Babylon was incorporated into the Persian Empire and for a time served as one of the winter capitals of the Persian kings. When Babylon finally rebelled against Xerxes (the Ahasuerus of the book of Esther) in 482 B.C., he put down the revolt with such violence that from that time forward, the city began to fade in importance. The first turn of the screw in Babylon's fall from power, however, occurred at the time of the Medo-Persian conquest in 539 B.C.

The book of Daniel integrates history and prophecy. The great lines of prophetic history Daniel outlined are rooted in the history of his time. The first world power of which the prophecies in Daniel, chapters 2 and 7, spoke was Babylon—represented by the head of gold in chapter 2 (vss. 32, 37) and by the lion in chapter 7 (vs. 4). Daniel himself lived under this world power of Babylon (chaps. 1–5, 7, 8), and he lived on to serve under Persian overlords as well (chaps. 6, 9–12). So Daniel himself saw the fulfillment of the first part of these great prophecies that God gave him.

Daniel acknowledged this transition of world empires in an interesting and subtle way in his words to Belshazzar that final night before Babylon's fall. He pointed out to Belshazzar that the king had "praised the gods of silver and gold, of bronze, iron, wood, and stone" (vs. 23). This sequence has a familiar sound to the reader of the prophecy given in Daniel 2. There the great image was made up of gold, silver, bronze, iron, and clay, followed by a great stone (vss. 31-35). Aside from the fact that Daniel has substituted "wood" for "clay," the sequence is the same in his words to Belshazzar on the night of the transition from the golden kingdom of Babylon to the silver empire of Medo-Persia. Daniel made an interesting variation here in chapter 5, however, for when he started to enumerate these metals, he put silver first, before the gold. Why the minor, but significant, alteration? Because the fulfillment of the prophecy given in chapter 2 was actually taking place that night; the silver was superseding the gold, and Daniel signifies this in his speech to the king.

Lessons of a Personal Nature

Deep spiritual truths of a personal nature can be found in this narrative apart from the historical and prophetic lessons present. We look back at Belshazzar with 20/20 hindsight and say, "What a foolish man! How could he have gone against the word of the prophet and the example of his grandfather Nebuchadnezzar's experience?"

Perhaps we should look at Belshazzar with a little more charity—not to excuse his blasphemy, but to take it to heart as an example for ourselves. Do we, too, fly in the face of the words of the prophets and the clear-cut examples of God's action in past history to cling stubbornly to our own ways? In our lives, have those words and actions fallen upon deaf ears and blind eyes? We may not be guilty of gross blasphemy and idolatry as was Belshazzar, but our own perverse ways can equally frustrate the grace of God.

Belshazzar spurned God's mercy and grace, extended to the royal house of Babylon since the time of Nebuchadnezzar. God's grace has also been extended to our forefathers, but that is not the issue. The issue is whether we have accepted God's grace for ourselves and have fashioned our lives according to it, rather than turning to our own ways. May God grant that the foolish example of Belshazzar will prevent our falling into similar ways today.

There are lessons of judgment in this chapter. God keeps accounts with nations and individuals. Babylon and Belshazzar were weighed in the balance of judgment and were found wanting (vs. 27). In one pan of the balances were placed God's mercy and righteousness; in the other, the rapacity, violence, and pride of Babylon and Belshazzar. The mercy of God far outweighed the pride of Belshazzar, but he chose not to accept that mercy. Judgment is not a popular topic in the modern world. At least not God's judgments. We want our fair share of justice in the courtroom, but when it comes to dealing with God, we would prefer a God who does not call us to account. We would rather evade our moral responsibility if at all possible. The topic of divine judgment was no more popular in the time of Daniel, Jeremiah, or Ezekiel than it is in our day. If the Old Testament prophets teach us anything, it is that in all ages a significant portion of God's people have tried to evade their moral responsibility and yet escape God's judgment.

Jesus illustrated the same thing in His parable of the rich man who tore down his barns to build bigger ones. This man lived his life according to the principle of greed. He wanted to merge more and more corporations. Then came the fateful night: "You fool! This very night your life will be demanded from you" (Luke 12:20). That was Belshazzar's condition as well. It could also be ours, but it need not be.

At the other extreme, we see the spiritual example of Daniel. He stood before the king confident in the God whom he served. He had received the word of the living God, therefore he did not need to fear the word of any king, regardless of how powerful he was. Whether he was honored with position (as he was by Nebuchadnezzar and Belshazzar), or cast into the den of lions (as he was by Darius), Daniel's faith and confidence in God remained strong. It mattered little to Daniel whether the Babylonians or the Persians controlled the world. Such details did not change his prayer habits or his personal integrity in the least. Regardless of how the political winds of the world blew, Daniel remained like the needle to the pole—faithful to his duty and to his God. Our example in chapter 5 is not Belshazzar, but Daniel. Belshazzar provides a warning of a path not to follow; Daniel stakes out the path of faith and trust that leads to the kingdom of God.

By faith, Daniel recognized that regardless of which armies were successful or which kingdoms were established at any particular moment, history was still under God's control. Ultimately, it was moving toward His goal. And his faith was realized when he saw the fulfillment of the very first step of the great prophecies as the Persians conquered Babylon.

We stand now at the other end of the line. In terms of Daniel 2, we stand at the very bottom of the image, among the feet and toes in the time of the iron and clay. We are waiting for the next and final step, the setting up of the stone kingdom, God's kingdom. We can look back over history and see that the beast-kingdoms of Daniel 7 have risen and fallen as God predicted. How much more, then, should we have faith and confidence in our God today, that He knows the future and has revealed it to His servants the prophets.

Lessons of a Historical Nature

Not only can we have confidence in the prophetic future as revealed to us through Daniel, but we can have confidence in the historical word that is conveyed to us in Daniel's book as well. Critics of the Bible have attempted to undermine the historical accuracy of Daniel and thus undermine his prophetic accuracy. The attempt has failed, and nowhere has it failed more than in chapter 5.

First, the critics denied that there even was such a person as Belshazzar. Then the tablets coming out of the mounds of Mesopotamia demonstrated his existence and his position and why the book of Daniel evaluated him the way it does.

A close examination of the historical setting of this chapter reveals just how precise and exact was the writer's knowledge of Babylon in the sixth century B.C. We can ask a very specific question of Daniel: "Who was the king in the palace the night that the city fell to the Persians?" This would be a good place to catch a writer of a later time in details of inaccurate knowledge. Based on the information preserved through classical historians, the answer would have been "Nabonidus." As the last known official king of Babylon, he should have been the monarch for whom Daniel interpreted the writing.

But the writer of Daniel did not erroneously put the well-known Nabonidus in the palace that night. Instead, he put the virtually unknown Belshazzar there. Daniel makes no mention of Nabonidus. If a banquet was held in the palace and Nabonidus was in the city, he certainly would have attended. Yet Daniel makes no mention of his presence. Why not? Where was Nabonidus? We did not know the answer to these questions until archaeologists dug up the tablet that we now know as the *Nabonidus Chronicle*. That tablet tells us clearly where Nabonidus was and why he was not in the city. He had taken another division of the Babylonian army out to the Tigris river where he fought Cyrus and his army in a nearby city named Opis. Two days before the city of Babylon fell, Nabonidus's army was defeated in the field by Cyrus's Persian troops. Nabonidus fled and did not return to the city of Babylon until well after the city was in Persian hands. So Daniel 5 is correct to ignore Nabonidus. He was not in Babylon the night it fell.

When Daniel came into the throne room of the palace that night, he saw a king. But that king was Belshazzar, not Nabonidus. How could Daniel have known that Belshazzar was in the palace that night, to protect the city, but that Nabonidus his father was absent? How could he have known these intimate details about the personnel present in the palace on that very night?

Only one answer to this question is possible. Daniel was an eye-witness to these events just as he tells us in his record. We may have confidence in the accuracy of the historical events described in the book of Daniel, and we may have confidence that the future events it predicts will come to pass.

Lessons of a Structural Nature

The portion of Daniel written in Aramaic covers chapters 2 through 7. At the very center of this section, chapters 4 and 5 deal with similar subjects—the king. In chapter 4, the king is Nebuchadnezzar; in chapter 5, the king is Belshazzar. Even though the events of these two chapters probably took place more than forty years apart, Daniel has chosen to tell these two stories side by side. He has deliberately arranged them in this way.

Although these two chapters both deal with the same type of sub-ject—the king—they deal with that subject in different ways. Those two treatments give us a picture of comparison and contrast which can influence the direction of our spiritual lives. In the end, Nebuchadnezzar provides us with a good example; Belshazzar never does. The first king came to a reluctant conversion; the second king refused to be converted at all.

To emphasize the similarities and the contrasts in these two his-torical narratives, Daniel located them at the center of the literary framework of this part of the book. As the center of the chiastic structure in Daniel, chapters 2 through 7, this arrangement focuses on individual responsibility. One king finally made a good choice, while the other king did not. The emphasis is on individual respon-sibility. Just as the monarchs of Babylon had an individual responsi-bility to God, so do each of us. We have a choice to make for or against God's grace and His kingdom. Although Belshazzar's example might urge us to delay and finally say No to God, Nebuchadnezzar's experience gives us motivation to meet and accept this true, per-sonal God and to enter His kingdom.

There may seem to be some distance between literary structure and personal spiritual lessons, but the form in which Daniel wrote and arranged his book emphasizes the fact that a close relationship actually exists between the two.

■ Applying the Word

Daniel 4, 5

1. Is the sin of Nebuchadnezzar in Daniel 4 a sin only of the rich and famous, or can I be guilty of the same sin? In what ways?
2. In what ways is my response to the message of God's prophets similar, or dissimilar, to Nebuchadnezzar's response to Daniel in chapter 4? What can I learn from Nebuchadnezzar's experience and response?
3. In what specific ways are the sins of Belshazzar, in chapter 5, similar to sins in my life? What can I learn from that chapter about responding to the lessons of history and the messages of God?
4. List the characteristics of Daniel brought to view in chapters 4 and 5. What can I learn from his example? What concrete things can I do today to put those lessons into practice?
5. What can I learn from these chapters about how the hand of God operates in human history? How can these inspired stories help me better understand the events I read about in the daily newspaper? Do these chapters indicate a divine pattern to history? In what way(s)?
6. Does my faith depend on whether the history given in these chapters is factually accurate? Why, or why not? If there were no such person as Belshazzar, would it make any difference to my understanding of Daniel's prophecies? In what way(s)?

■ Researching the Word

1. With the help of a concordance, find and list all the references in the Bible to the word "times" as a prophetic time period. Also find and list all the references to the prophetic

time periods of 1,260 days and 42 months. How are these three time periods related? What evidence do you have for your answer? You may find it helpful to study *The Seventh-day Adventist Bible Commentary* on the passages referring to these time periods as you seek to flesh out your understanding of this prophetic element.

2. Daniel 4 completes Nebuchadnezzar's story. Go over the first four chapters, and develop a composite biographical sketch of the man. Draw a line down the center of a page in your Daniel notebook. On one side list Nebuchadnezzar's strengths; on the other side list his weaknesses. What evidence of spiritual growth do you find in these chapters? You may want to compare your findings with the article on Nebuchadnezzar in a Bible encyclopedia, Bible dictionary, or some other reference work.

■ Further Study of the Word

1. For more on the gradual discovery of Belshazzar, see F. D. Nichol, ed., *The Seventh-day Adventist Commentary*, 4:806-808.
2. For more on the history of Babylon, see S. H. Horn, et al., *The Seventh-day Adventist Bible Dictionary*, 108, 109.
3. For more on Nebuchadnezzar's madness in extrabiblical texts, see S. H. Horn, "New Light on Nebuchadnezzar's Madness," *Ministry*, April 1978, 38-40.
4. For further study of Daniel 4, read E. G. White, *Prophets and Kings*, 514-521; and M. Maxwell, *God Cares*, 1:57-71.
5. For further study of Daniel 5, read E. G. White, *Prophets and Kings*, 522-538; and M. Maxwell, *God Cares*, 1:77-89.

CHAPTER FOUR

Kingly Persecution

Daniel 3, 6

The particular experiences of the Hebrew exiles in Babylon singled out in these two chapters begin on a very negative note, but they end with a glorious and miraculous deliverance in both cases. In the first, the trial involves Daniel's three friends (chap. 3). The second involves Daniel himself (chap. 6).

People often wonder where Daniel was while his friends were undergoing their test on the plain of Dura. We don't know the answer to this question, because the text simply doesn't tell us. Common speculation is that Daniel was absent on an errand for the king. That is a reasonable suggestion, but we do not know for sure why Daniel wasn't present when the king set up his image. What we do know is that Daniel himself later faced the same kind of test. He did not have to suffer with his friends on the plain of Dura, but he did not escape persecution. In chapter 3, Daniel's companions face the fiery furnace, but in chapter 6, Daniel faces the den of lions.

These two stories contain a number of common features. Both start with an experience of persecution by the king who was reigning at the time—Nebuchadnezzar in the first instance, and Darius the Mede in the second. Both stories tell of the faithful courage of the Hebrews and their trust in God in spite of the circumstances. Both tell how the Hebrew exiles were plunged into trials that were intended to take their lives. Both stories tell of a miraculous deliverance. And in both cases, the king involved recognized the Hebrews' faithfulness to the true God as illustrated by their deliverance.

Not only do these two chapters deal with similar themes, they are also placed at complementary locations in the literary structure of Daniel's book. As we have seen earlier, the literary structure of the historical section of Daniel is carefully constructed to bring out the similarities between the chapters that are paired together due to common themes. In the case of chapters 3 and 6, the common themes are persecution and ultimate victory through faithfulness to God.

As has been noted before, the historical section of Daniel (2–7) was written in Aramaic, thus setting it off from the rest of the book. Likewise, the narratives in that section were arranged in a chiastic order in which paired narratives were located at similar junctures in that structure. In the preceding chapter, we saw that chapters 4 and 5, dealing with the theme of fallen kings, comprise the two central narratives of this historical section. We come now to chapters 3 and 6—the intermediate narratives in this chiastic arrangement. The final part of this chiastic outline is treated in the next chapter of this book which examines chapters 2 and 7 in terms of their description of fallen kingdoms.

■ Getting Into the Word

Daniel 3

Read Daniel 3 two times. Then work out answers to the following questions and issues, recording your conclusions in your Daniel notebook.

1. Describe the event taking place on the plain of Dura. Who was invited, and what might be the probable reason for the event? The ending of chapter 2 will help in understanding why Daniel's friends were there.
2. Why do you think Nebuchadnezzar went to the trouble of erecting the great image? What can we learn from Daniel 2 about the symbolism of the metal used for the image in Daniel 3? Why did Nebuchadnezzar insist that everyone bow down to the image? What was the meaning behind bowing to the image?
3. List as many factors as you can find in chapter 3 that indi-

cate pressure being put on the three Hebrews to conform.
Why didn't they bow down? Do the Ten Commandments
relate to their predicament? If so, how? What is the relationship between the first and the second commandments?
How does that relationship parallel what Nebuchadnezzar
was requesting of his officers?

4. List as many factors as you can find in chapter 3 that indicate how the Hebrews found the spiritual fortitude to resist
the king's order. What light does chapter 2 throw on the
source of their courage? List and analyze the different elements in the three Hebrews' courageous response when
they reject the king's order to bow down. What is the significance of each?

5. What can we learn about Nebuchadnezzar from Daniel 3?
What is the significance of the chapter's conclusion?

■ Exploring the Word

The Test

Nebuchadnezzar ordered that a great image be set up on the plain
of Dura (3:1). Considerable confusion has existed about exactly what
and where Dura was.

Scholars used to think Dura was the name of a city somewhere in
the kingdom of Babylon. Identifying such a city, however, has been
difficult. Another suggestion has been that Dura was the name of an
irrigation canal and that the plain of Dura was located close by. This
suggestion has not worked out well either, so a search has been made
in another direction.

Some refinements have been made recently in identifying the location of the plain of Dura. The name *Dura* is also the simple
Babylonian word for a "wall." *Dur* is the word for "wall," and the
letter *a* at the end of the word is the article "the" in Aramaic. So
translating this phrase directly, instead of leaving it as an unknown
place name, indicates that Nebuchadnezzar set up his image on "the
plain of the wall."

But the question remains: "What plain and what wall?" There were two major walls surrounding the city of Babylon (see the map of Babylon, page 79). The inner wall, about a mile long on each side, surrounded the central part of the city. The territory inside this inner wall was urban, containing many buildings and streets along with the palace and the largest temple in the city.

Later, Nebuchadnezzar added an outer wall several miles long that extended to the east bank of the Euphrates River and around the city. In Nebuchadnezzar's time, Babylonian engineers and builders had not yet filled this area between the inner and outer walls with buildings, although construction was taking place. The open area served as a parade ground for the army and a place within the city walls where the troops could bivouac. This large open space between the two walls could properly be called the "plain of the wall," or "the plain of Dura." In all likelihood this was where the events of chapter 3 took place.

Such a location would have facilitated attendance at this great assembly by officials from Babylon (vs. 3). It would also have put the image close to the palace of the king. There is no reason to suppose that the assembly gathered at some site in the kingdom remote from the capital.

Another consideration is the great size of the image. Its measurements are interesting from several points of view. Daniel says the image was sixty cubits high and six cubits wide (vs. 1). The Babylonians employed a sexagesimal mathematical system based on the number six, unlike our decimal system based on the number ten. So the measurements Daniel gives are typically Babylonian. But some have objected that an image sixty cubits high and only six cubits wide would be too tall for its width. A 1:10 ratio would look very skinny.

It's true that such measurements would result in a very tall, thin statue. Yet the ancients depicted their gods exactly this way. The figurines of Baal that come mainly from Syria and Palestine are good examples. The arms, legs, and bodies of these figurines are long and spindly, what we would call a matchstick kind of image. So for Nebuchadnezzar to make a statue with these proportions would not have been unusual.

What *was* unusual was the image's height. Some have objected that Nebuchadnezzar would not have made a figure so tall and that the sixty-cubit height (approximately ninety feet) is an exaggeration belonging to legend rather than historical fact. However, some examples of similarly tall statues can be cited in the ancient world. Probably the most famous of these was the colossus that stood on the island of Rhodes. At seventy cubits, it actually stood ten cubits higher than Nebuchadnezzar's image. The colossi of Memnon at Thebes in southern Egypt consist of two representations of the king Amenhotep III, one of which still stands to a height of sixty-five feet. So although Nebuchadnezzar's image would have been exceptionally tall, such statues were by no means unknown in the ancient world. As a modern comparison, it is interesting to note that the figure of the Statue of Liberty, excluding the pedestal, stands twenty feet higher than did Nebuchadnezzar's image.

Another factor to consider in terms of the height of this image is the height of another structure that may have been in the area. If Nebuchadnezzar set up his image in the plain between the city walls, and if it faced west, it would have been looking at the old central city of Babylon. In the center of the city was the temple area of Marduk, which contained the great temple tower, or ziggurat, of Babylon. At some 300 feet high, it dominated the landscape. Its base was approximately 300 feet square and extended upward in a solid pyramid shape through seven levels, each covered with enamel bricks of a different color from the previous level. The top level consisted of a temple to the god Marduk in addition to the main temple located at the foot of the ziggurat. With such a monumental structure nearby, Nebuchadnezzar's image, standing a "mere" ninety feet high, would not appear so exceptional.

Who or What Did Nebuchanezzar's Image Represent?

Basically, there are two possibilities. Either it represented a god or it represented a man. If the image was designed to represent a man, no doubt that man was Nebuchadnezzar himself. If it represented a god, it most likely represented Marduk, the city and national god of Babylon and the personal god of Nebuchadnezzar.

Which of these two possibilities is more likely? Daniel 3 does not tell us precisely what the image represented, but it does tell us that the assembled crowd was to bow down and "worship" the image (vss. 7, 12, 14, 15). Although the citizens of the kingdom were expected to perform obeisance to the kings of Babylon, they did not worship them. In Egypt, the kings were considered to be gods, but in Mesopotamia, kings were only the special servants of the gods. Only a very few Mesopotamian kings claimed to be divine, and Nebuchadnezzar was not among them. In fact, Babylonian theology held that it was a sin for the king to claim divinity and that those who did so would be punished by the gods. So it is considerably more likely that the image was intended to represent Marduk, the god of Babylon, than Nebuchadnezzar.

Why did Nebuchadnezzar have this image erected? Again, Daniel 3 does not tell us. But it is easy to see a connection between chapters 2 and 3. In chapter 2 the king dreamed of a great image made of different metals that represented the successive kingdoms that would rule over the earth. The immediate meaning of this dream to Nebuchadnezzar was that another kingdom would follow Babylon (vs. 39). This was not good news to Babylon's king! Hitler thought that the Third Reich would stand for a thousand years, and Nebuchadnezzar probably had a similar future in mind for his kingdom. In Daniel 2:32, 36-39, Babylon is represented as the golden part of the image. Thus by making an image similar to the one he had seen in his dream, but by making it all of gold (probably gold foil sheathing a wooden form underneath), the king denied the dream's meaning—the succession of kingdoms that was to follow Babylon on the world stage. In Nebuchadnezzar's thinking, Babylon was to stand forever. Constructing an image all of gold represented that fact.

However, there probably was more to the erection of the image than just a response by the king to the message of his dream. The Babylonian Chronicle proves helpful at this point. Prior to the discovery of these tablets containing the official record of

Nebuchadnezzar's kingship, scholars thought that his lengthy forty-three-year rule was a monolithic, unchallenged reign. But the Chronicle tells a different story. In fact, there was such serious opposition to Nebuchadnezzar that on one occasion a revolt arose from within the city that resulted in hand-to-hand combat in the very palace itself with the king fighting for his life! The Chronicle entry reads:

> In the tenth year [595/594 B.C.] the king of Akkad [Babylon] was in his own land; from the month of Kislev [December] to the month of Tebet [January] there was rebellion in Akkad. . . . With arms he [the king] slew many of his own army. His own hand captured his enemy (quoted in Wiseman, *Chronicles of Chaldean Kings*, 73).

Daniel does not give a date for the events of chapter 3. But it is tempting to link them to the rebellion described in the Babylonian Chronicle and to see in the king's demand that all the officials of the kingdom bow down to the image, a loyalty oath required in response to the problem of disloyalty in their ranks. If this speculation is correct, then the Babylonian Chronicle provides a possible date for the events described in Daniel 3. If the rebellion took place in 594 B.C., then the episode with the image could have taken place later that year or early the next year as a response to the rebellion.

Continuing that hypothesis, it is important to note who was present at the dedication of the great image. Not all the citizens of Babylon were called to assemble. It was a select group, identified as "the satraps, prefects, governors, advisers, treasurers, judges, magistrates and all other provincial officials" (vss. 2, 3). These Babylonian government officials were "summoned" (vs. 2) by the king to attend the dedication ceremony. If the summons was a response to the rebellion that had taken place, it is easy to see why the king would have selected this group. Government officials and those working in the palace were the most likely to formulate plots against the king. They were the ones potentially most dangerous to him, and they were also the ones whose support was most crucial to the king. Any disloyalty in this group would plunge the monarch and his kingdom into serious trouble again.

To prevent such a development, the king assembled these officials and had them swear an oath of allegiance. It took a religious form. If one bows down and worships the god of Babylon, then one is also pledging allegiance to faithfully serve that god and his earthly representative, the king. Thus the events of chapter 3 can be seen as preventive politics practiced in religious garb on the plain of Dura.

The demand to worship the image was not specifically targeted at Daniel's three Hebrew friends. They were simply caught up in the situation because they were civil servants of the government of Babylon—positions for which they had been brought as exiles to Babylon from Judah and to which they had been appointed by the end of chapter 2 (see verse 49).

Like them, we, too, may be carried along by the force of circumstances over which we have no direct control. There comes a time, however, when those who follow God have to take a stand for the right and be counted. We cannot always flow with the crowd, no matter how tempting it may be to do so. One lesson from chapter 3 is that faith in the true God will bring us through such trials, just as it did the three Hebrews facing the king's anger on the plain of Dura.

The Response

Heralds instructed the assembled officials to bow down and worship the great image when the players in the orchestra struck up their music. And with the exception of the three Hebrews, that is exactly what they did (vss. 4-7).

We do not know how many persons gathered before the image, but the list of officials given in verse 2 seems to be all-inclusive. Perhaps 2,000 officials would have been involved. Imagine that large crowd of 2,000 people all bowing down at one time. Then imagine the three Hebrews standing all alone as everybody else was prostrate on the ground. These three men must have felt very much alone as they stood out distinctly from the bowing multitude. They felt keenly the pressure of 2,000 other officials all conforming, all obeying the king's decree. Some of these officials probably worked with Shadrach, Meshach, and Abednego. They may even have been friends. Can't you imagine an official who is bowing near these three Hebrews whispering, "Get down! Get down, for your own good! You don't have to mean it; just get down!"

But the Hebrews did not flinch or bow. They were not swayed by the crowd, all of whom were bowing before the image. There are times when Christians, like these men, have to take an unpopular stand. Early Christians refused to burn incense to the emperor, and in some instances it cost them their lives. Burning incense to the emperor was an act of worship; bowing down on the plain of Dura was also an act of worship. Worshipers of the true God could not participate in either ceremony.

No doubt, the pressure the three Hebrews felt from the conforming crowd intensified when they were brought before the king (vs. 13). Nebuchadnezzar was the world's most powerful monarch. Whatever he wanted to do with them, would be done; they were completely in his control. There was one thing, however, he could not do. He could not violate their will and choice. He could attempt to persuade them. He could try to coerce them. He could punish them. But he could not force them to act against their will.

One or more furnaces probably stood nearby, adding to the monarch's threat. We must not think these were constructed specially for the Hebrews when it was discovered that they would not obey the king and worship the image. Rather, the furnaces had been constructed in advance and were standing ready for anyone foolish enough to resist the king's loyalty oath. As the music played and the Hebrews remained standing, they could look out over the huge crowd bowing to the ground and see clearly the instruments of punishment for those who refused.

Most likely, these furnaces were brick kilns. Bricks were made in two ways in ancient times—by drying them in the sun and by firing them in kilns. Kiln-fired bricks were harder and were used especially for the outer surfaces of buildings. The great plain between the two sets of city walls was a place of ongoing construction projects, and the main construction material used was not wood or cement, but clay. The city of Babylon was made of thousands, if not millions, of clay bricks. The kilns used to fire these bricks were shaped like a beehive with a hole at the top of the cone through which flammable material was dropped; there was another tunnel-like opening on one side. Pallets of bricks were put in the side opening, and the material with which the kiln was fired was dropped into the kiln from above. Steps went up the side of the kiln to the upper opening. The Hebrews were probably dropped into the kiln through the hole at the top.

The kilns were probably already fired up by the time the ceremony took place. Thus the Hebrews not only knew they would be thrown into one of these kilns for their refusal to worship the image, they could actually see it burning and smoking in the distance. But in spite of looking right into the terrifying face of their fate, they stood firm in their refusal to bow down (vss. 16-18). Fear of a horrible death could not induce them to be unfaithful to God!

It's also interesting that they didn't break ranks over this issue. Two didn't stand firm with one bowing. Two didn't give in and leave the third alone in his faithfulness to God. All three were united in the common bond of faith and courage so that when one spoke to the king, he spoke for all three. This is the kind of unity in the faith that is needed as the church approaches its final crisis. When Christians break ranks and divide in their response over test and trial, they only make it harder for themselves and for their fellow Christians.

The king was already angry, and he was getting progressively more so. Upon hearing that the three Hebrews had disobeyed his order, he was "furious with rage" (vs. 13). When they rejected a second opportunity to bow down to the image, "his attitude toward them changed" and he became even more "furious with Shadrach, Meshach and Abednego" (vs. 19). It's not a good thing to have the world's most powerful ruler angry at you, with his instruments of torture and annihilation standing by at the ready.

Why was the king so enraged? As a matter of policy, Assyrians and Babylonians did not force captive peoples to convert to the worship of their conqueror's gods. Why didn't Nebuchadnezzar have more tolerance for these Hebrews who didn't choose to worship his god?

Something more is involved here. If the scenario suggested earlier is correct and the events of chapter 3 are seen in terms of a recent revolt in Babylon, then we can understand why the king would have been so upset with these officials who would not take his loyalty oath. In Nebuchadnezzar's mind, here were the seeds of another revolt in the making. No wonder this was such a sensitive issue with him and that he took the Hebrews' refusal so seriously.

Yet, in spite of all this, the king was still willing to give them another opportunity to bow to the image. He was willing to have the orchestra strike up again and see if the Hebrews would obey (vs. 15). But their mind was set so firmly upon remaining faithful to God that they told the king not even to bother with another stanza of music. Their decision was set in a cement stronger than that which held the city's walls together. They put it this way:

> O Nebuchadnezzar, we do not need to defend ourselves before you in this matter. If we are thrown into the blazing furnace, the God we serve is able to save us from it, and he will rescue us from your hand, O king. But even if he does not, we want you to know, O king, that we will not serve your gods or worship the image of gold you have set up (vss. 16-18).

This was a death-before-dishonor response, but it was more. They clearly enunciated the reason they could not obey. It sprang from "the God we serve." They served Yahweh (Jehovah), not Marduk. Their refusal to bow to Nebuchadnezzar's image involved more than just the refusal of these three men to obey the order of one king. Two gods were involved—Marduk and Yahweh. Nebuchadnezzar served Marduk; the three Hebrews served Yahweh. The scene on the plain thus became a contest between the true God and the false god, played out through their human representatives.

From all appearances, it looked as though the Hebrews were the certain losers in this contest; in actuality, they were in a win-win situation. If they died as a consequence of their steadfast trust in

God, they could be seen as martyrs courageous enough to die for their faith. If, on the other hand, their God did deliver them—as they stated in their second option—then His glory and honor would be made even more manifest. But this does not subtract in the least from the courage and faithfulness they demonstrated. As far as they knew, they were about to die when they told the king they did not need a second chance to bow to the image. Their reply is a remarkable testimony to their faith and trust and courage.

Their example raises a question for us: Is our faith and trust in God strong enough that we would be able to stand up to such a test and exhibit the spiritual courage they showed? Are we sufficiently grounded in His Word and in our experiences with Him that we, too, could stand before a king and declare that under no circumstance would we dishonor the God who has loved us?

Sometime in the future we may indeed have to face such a test. For the present, however, our lives are confronted with lesser challenges. How we respond to these prepares us for greater tests. They indicate how we will respond when larger issues arise. The Bible has a principle of spiritual life that applies here: "Whoever can be trusted with very little can also be trusted with much" (Luke 16:10). The wear and tear of ordinary, everyday life are directly related to the great challenges of life. God prepares us to meet the great trials of life in the everyday school of hard knocks. Moses spent forty years in the wilderness tending sheep, but it was that preparation that enabled him to meet with Pharaoh on equal terms. We, too, can develop a spiritual preparation for whatever life may hold for us.

The Result

Nebuchadnezzar was not happy with the response of the three Hebrews. The punishment previously designed was not sufficient in the face of such insolence. He ordered that the furnace be heated seven times hotter (vs. 19). How would he have accomplished this? Remember, this took place in Babylon. Today we call this area Iraq. Iraq is a country rich in oil. Most of that oil is underground and has to be pumped out by modern oil companies. But there are places where oil seeps to the surface. These open asphalt wells have been used in modern times, and they were known and used in ancient times as well. The best way to have a brick kiln heated to a much higher temperature would be to throw some petroleum into it.

The king's order to increase the temperature was obeyed, and it succeeded so well that the men who carried the three bound Hebrews up the steps on the side of the furnace and threw them in, were themselves killed by the blast of the furnace (vs. 22). If the overheated furnace did that to the men who threw the Hebrews in, you can imagine what it would do to the Hebrews themselves who were directly in the furnace itself. But it didn't. The king came over to see how the punishment was progressing. He probably bent down to look in the tunnel at the side of the kiln. He expected to see the charred and burning bodies of his three unfaithful officials; instead he saw them perfectly unharmed and unburned! The three men had been firmly tied when they were thrown into the furnace (vs. 23). Now as the king looked in, they were unbound and walking around in the fire! When they finally came out of the kiln, the report was, "the fire had not harmed their bodies, nor was a hair of their heads singed; their robes were not scorched, and there was no smell of fire on them" (vs. 27).

This was a very selective fire! It had burned the ropes right off the Hebrews' wrists. It had even burned the men who had thrown them into the fire. But it did not touch the bodies of these three men, nor their garments, nor even a single hair of their heads! There was no smell of smoke about them! It was as if they had never been in the fire at all. It was as if there was a kind of protective non-flammable envelope surrounding them. Thus God honored the faith and trust of His faithful servants.

From that dramatic answer to prayer, we can see that we serve a prayer-answering God. He may not answer our prayers in such a dramatic way, but the fact that He did so for Shadrach, Meshach, and Abednego assures us that He will hear and answer our prayers in the way that He sees is best.

Our prayers should express the same confidence and faith that the prayers of these three Hebrews did. They did not demand a single, specific answer from God; they recognized the possibilities and left the decision to God. He can deliver us and will do so if He sees best; but He may also answer No. In such cases, we should be willing to accept that answer and live with it—or die with it, as Shadrach, Meshach, and Abednego were ready to do. Their example is an example of faith and courage to us, but it is also an example of accepting God's will.

As recorded in the Gospels, the miracles Jesus performed had an additional purpose beyond benefitting specific individuals. They were also teaching vehicles designed to convey a spiritual lesson. For example, Jesus performed seven miracles on Sabbath. These not only blessed those who were involved, they also taught something about the Sabbath. They taught that Jesus was Lord of the Sabbath and that the Sabbath could be used for His purposes in the healing and salvation of mankind (see Matthew 12:8). They also taught that He was the Creator and re-Creator (see John 5, 7). Likewise, the miracle God performed for the three Hebrews in the fiery furnace had a purpose beyond their deliverance. Through this miracle, Nebuchadnezzar and the hundreds or thousands of Babylonian officials on the plain of Dura were brought face to face with the true God of heaven.

Nebuchadnezzar understood the lesson and said so. As he looked into the fire and saw Shadrach, Meshach, and Abednego unharmed, he addressed them as "servants of the Most High God" (vs. 26). The king even decreed that all those in the nations he ruled should honor the God who had so dramatically demonstrated His power to deliver His servants—thus ensuring that the miraculous event would be known throughout his empire (vss. 28, 29).

But God did not leave it to chance that Nebuchadnezzar would understand clearly who had performed this miracle. As the king looked into the fire, he saw the three Hebrews walking about unharmed in the flames, but he also saw a fourth being in the fire with them. He immediately recognized this figure as divine—a "son of the gods" (vs. 25). Later, he identified this divine being as an angel (vs. 28). We must not suppose that Nebuchadnezzar identified this fourth person with God's Son in the sense that we Christians think of Jesus Christ today. Remember that the king was still in his pagan, unconverted state at this time. This is clear from the way he commanded all his officials at the beginning of this narrative to bow down to the image of his god. It is also clear in his response to Shadrach, Meshach, and Abednego when they refused to bow to the image because they served another God. Clearly, this miraculous deliverance made a deep impression upon Nebuchadnezzar and caused him to recognize the superiority of the Hebrews' God. But he was not converted to serve their God at this time. This experience surely helped prepare him for such a conversion, but that experience was not complete until the end of his seven years of insanity described in Daniel 4. Not until then did Nebuchadnezzar come to accept the true God whom he called the God Most High (vss. 34-37).

Nebuchadnezzar did not see a clear picture of the Messiah in the fourth figure walking about in the fire. He recognized this being as a "son of the gods" (vs. 25), as his description can be most literally and accurately translated. This is not at all the same as "the Son of God." A "son of the gods" simply means a being from the realm of the gods, that is a supernatural being. His identification of this being as an angel brings up the references to other angels in the book of Daniel. Two of them are named Gabriel and Michael. Gabriel was the one who brought some of the prophecies to Daniel (9:21, 23). Michael, the archangel (or prince of the heavenly princes, 8:11, 25; 10:13; 12:1) was the one who stood up for and defended the people of God, both in Babylonian and Persian times and at the end of time (10:13; 12:1). Given the defensive posture in which we find Michael, he would have been the ideal angel to have protected and defended the three Hebrews in the fire. From a New Testament perspective, we know that Michael is Christ (Rev. 12:7), but that would not necessarily have been evident to Nebuchadnezzar on this occasion. He simply knew that the God of the Hebrews had sent a divinelike being to rescue them. That very vivid impression would have been adequate for the time being in the course of Nebuchadnezzar's spiritual pilgrimage.

An interesting contrast is involved here when one compares the concluding scene of the vision of Daniel 7. There Daniel looked into the heavenly courts and saw the Ancient of Days, God the Father, conducting the heavenly tribunal. At the conclusion of that scene, one like a "son of man . . . approached the Ancient of Days" (7:13) to receive the kingdom. The language here is similar to Nebuchadnezzar's pronouncement in chapter 3:25, but there is a contrast as well. In chapter 3 we see one like "a son of the gods" here on earth, a divinelike being come down from heaven to earth. In chapter 7 we see one like "a son of man" in heaven, a humanlike incarnate being who has entered heaven where He will receive the kingdom for ever and ever. Michael is the protector of His people here on earth, and He will be their great ruler here for all eternity. He is none other than Jesus Christ who will come again at last as King of kings and Lord of lords to fulfill the prediction of Daniel 7:14 and Revelation 19:16.

■ Getting Into the Word

Daniel 6

Read Daniel 6 through at least two times. Then complete the following exercises in your Daniel notebook.

1. What can you learn from Daniel 6 about the way the Persians set up their new administration in the recently conquered province of Babylon? What part did Daniel play in that administrative organization?
2. What attributes of Daniel's character can you infer from the information given in chapter 6? List them in your notebook. What does this chapter tell you about Daniel's spiritual practices? How were they affected by external circumstances?
3. Was Daniel right in making an issue of his spiritual practices? Could he have avoided trouble by continuing his prayer life in private without publicly disregarding the ban against prayer? What was the motivation of his enemies?
4. According to chapter 6, what kind of person was Darius the

Mede? What evidence do you find in this chapter of a change in his personal spiritual experience? If so, what direction does it take? Summarize your conclusions in your Daniel notebook.

5. What similarities and differences do you find between God's deliverance of Shadrach, Meshach, and Abednego in chapter 3 and His deliverance of Daniel in chapter 6? List them in separate columns in your Daniel notebook.

■ Exploring the Word

The Setting

The events recorded in Daniel 5 and 6 took place within a relatively short period of time spanning the fall of Babylon and the short-term aftermath of that conquest by the Persians. Chapter 5 describes the kingdom's collapse from the Babylonian viewpoint of what was going on within the city and the palace. Chapter 6 recounts what took place soon after, as the Persians set up their administration of the newly conquered territories. Daniel played a part both in the final events under the last Babylonian king, Belshazzar, and in the setting up of the new Persian administration. In fact, he played a prominent part in that transition. Unfortunately, it was his prominence that got him into difficulty.

In the ancient world, the Persians were fairly benevolent conquerors. For example, they commonly, though not always, left in place the indigenous rulers and officials of conquered territories. Instead of removing them, they adapted them to their use. Sometimes, this applied even to conquered kings who were left to rule their previous holdings under the authority of the Persian Empire. Another evidence of Persian benevolence was their return of captive peoples to their homelands. As the books of Ezra and Nehemiah make plain, it was under Persian kings that the people of Judah were allowed to return home.

The Persians did not extend preferential treatment to the kings of Babylon, however. Belshazzar was killed the night the city was taken; the Persians captured his father Nabonidus and exiled him to faraway Carmania. Actually, exile was probably an act of kindness, for Nabonidus could easily have been executed.

With Belshazzar and Nabonidus both out of the picture and the kingdom taken over by the Persians, it was necessary to appoint a new person to head up the Persian government of Babylon. Cyrus, the ruler of the empire, appointed Darius the Mede to this job. Darius was to rule in Babylon as a vassal king subject to Cyrus, who continued to rule the Persian Empire of which Babylon was now a part.

At this juncture we encounter a historical question: Who was this person called Darius the Mede in Daniel 6? No one by that name is known from secular sources of the time.

A number of suggestions have been made regarding the identity of this biblical Darius, but no consensus has yet been reached. Those who accept the historicity of Daniel 6, all accept the premise that "Darius" is the throne name of someone who was known by a different, personal name before being appointed to the rulership of Babylon. Such a solution would not be unusual. The practice of assuming a throne name at the time of accession was well known throughout the ancient Near East. In Egypt, kings took on a whole set of five different names when they succeeded to the throne. In Mesopotamia, two Assyrian kings who conquered the city of Babylon and placed themselves upon its throne assumed throne names when they did so. Tiglath-pileser III assumed the throne name of Pulu (both names are used in 2 Kings 15:19, 29), and Shalmaneser V was known by the throne name of Ululaia.

In Judah we have the clear case of the leper-king Uzziah who was also known by the name of Azariah (2 Kings 15:1; 2 Chron. 26:1). Azariah was probably his original name and Uzziah his throne name. It is also possible that Jedidiah was Solomon's personal name (2 Sam. 12:25), and the latter his throne name—or the reverse. Some historians of Persia have suggested that the names by which the famous Persian kings are known—Cyrus, Darius, Xerxes—may have been throne names and that they had other personal names before they became king. Therefore, the suggestion that "Darius the Mede" is a throne name used in the book of Daniel reflects a well-known practice in the ancient world.

What is more difficult is the task of identifying the individual who bore this throne name. Darius the Mede should not be confused with Darius I Hystaspes, also known as "Darius the Great," who ruled Persia from 522 to 486 B.C. This individual came from a Persian, not Median, line and ruled later than the Darius of Daniel 6. The readings suggested at the end of this chapter discuss in detail the different suggestions that have been made for identifying the historical person Daniel 6 refers to as "Darius the Mede."

The Plot

From the point of view of Daniel's book, what Darius *does* is more important than who Darius *is*. It's important to note that Daniel was not originally singled out for punishment or persecution. Instead, the Persians intimately involved him in their reorganization of the government of the province of Babylon. Darius had appointments to make on two different levels of officialdom. One hundred twenty lower-level officials needed to be appointed or confirmed in office, and three officials were to be installed on the highest level. Daniel was one of these three uppermost administrators, and Darius was soon to consider making him the most preeminent of the three (6:1-3). This would have been equivalent to making Daniel the chief governor of all Babylon.

Naturally, his civil-service colleagues reacted negatively to Daniel's impending elevation. They were jealous and set out to make sure that he didn't receive this highest post. The plot they hatched centered on Daniel's religious practices, because they knew that this was the only "flaw" they could exploit. He was so conscientious in all the affairs he carried out for the king that these jealous colleagues knew they would never catch him in rank dishonesty or inefficiency (vss. 4, 6). So they set a religious trap for Daniel. They approached the king with a proposal. "The king should issue an edict," they urged, "and enforce the decree that anyone who prays to any god or man during the next thirty days, except to you, O king, shall be thrown into the lions' den" (vss. 6, 7).

Now this is a very strange-sounding request. One might well ask, "What about the other gods of Babylon?"

In order to understand the appeal of such a decree, one needs to understand the disturbed religious conditions in Babylon immediately after the Persian conquest. Nabonidus, the last Babylonian king, set out to protect the city of Babylon as the final bastion of defense against the Persians. He attempted to do so not only with troops and arms, but also with the help of the gods. His representatives went to the major cities of Babylonia and took the images of their gods out of the temples and brought them to Babylon. The rationale was that by gathering the images of the gods in Babylon, the gods themselves would be obliged to defend the city. Nabonidus wanted the gods on his side.

The Persians were successful in spite of this ploy, of course. But when they took over, they faced not only political problems; they faced a religious problem as well. With the images of the gods gathered in the capital city, people throughout the kingdom were having difficulty praying in empty temples. The Persians set about to rectify this situation by sending the gods back to their respective cities and temples, but the logistics and the ritual that had to take place made it certain that the transfer would take some time to accomplish. Not until the end of the Babylonian calendar year, some four months later, did all the gods find their way back to their locations, says the Nabonidus Chronicle.

Under such confused conditions, a request to divert prayers away from any god except the king himself becomes easier to understand. During more normal times, such a request would have bordered on the absurd, but these were not normal times either religiously or politically.

The Babylonian officials who proposed this regulation were not actually concerned whether someone prayed to these other gods. They were interested in only one God—Yahweh, or Jehovah, the God to whom Daniel prayed. They took advantage of the times in order to devise a plot to bring Daniel down. They knew how regular he was in his prayer habits. Three times a day, Daniel prayed to his God, facing west toward Jerusalem where the temple had once stood (vs. 10). Daniel probably prayed at the times when the morning and evening sacrifices would have been offered in that temple had it still been standing (9:21).

Daniel didn't flaunt his prayers in a display of superficial religiosity, but neither did he try to hide these personal spiritual exercises. His fellow officials knew his habits well. They knew how regular and faithful he was in this practice. They also knew that he was a man of such integrity and faithfulness to his God that he would not interrupt his prayer life simply because of a mere human prohibition. Daniel had faith in his God, but his colleagues had faith in Daniel!

Their confidence in Daniel's steadfastness is a remarkable example to us of faithful devotion. If we were to find ourselves in a situation similar to that in which Daniel found himself, would others feel sure that our steadfastness would not change? Daniel's vibrant, active faith found its source in his regular time for prayer and devotions. He didn't start praying only when some crisis came along. Nor was he engaging in some spiritual showmanship by continuing his prayers in spite of the decree. Although his prayers may have become more fervent as a result of the king's decree, Daniel's basic relationship with God had already been established in the habits of life. Long before this plot was formed against him, he had found prayer to be the vital ingredient in his busy life in Babylon as a high-ranking official. The decree simply brought to the forefront the habits of a lifetime on the part of this faithful servant of God.

How Long Had Daniel Been Praying Like This?

He was deported to Babylon in 605 B.C. when he was approximately eighteen years of age. The present episode took place during the brief reign of Darius the Mede, therefore it must have taken place either in 539 B.C. or 538 B.C. If we add Daniel's sixty-seven years in Babylon to his age of eighteen when taken captive, we come to an age of about eighty-five years for Daniel at the time this episode occurred. Daniel was an old man when the Persians took over, but he was still intellectually capable, and his life of faith still burned bright. This was the result of a lifetime of faith and prayer, a beautiful example of faithfulness.

Daniel's faithfulness did not go unnoticed by God. On two different occasions, an angel was sent to him and addressed him in these words: "O Daniel, man greatly beloved" (Dan. 9:23; 10:10, KJV; "highly" or "greatly" esteemed, NIV). God had not forgotten His servant simply because he was an old man. On the contrary, His regard for Daniel grew even greater as the man grew older in the faith and came to know God better. This should come as an encouragement to those who have grown older. Companions and relatives on earth may forget, but God never forgets. Daniel's case demonstrates the divine concern.

The decree was to cover a span of thirty days during which no one was to pray to anyone other than Darius (6:7). Daniel's enemies didn't have to wait this whole time to see whether Daniel would violate the new command. They undoubtedly caught him praying on the first or second day. So they rushed off to the king and told him of Daniel's disregard for his decree.

Now the laws of the Persians were irrevocable (vs. 15). Having once been enacted, the decree could not be changed to fit the new circumstances. Daniel, a favorite of the king, had been caught in the king's own ordinance. And the king had been caught in the scheme of the officials plotting against Daniel. He tried all day to work out some sort of arrangement whereby Daniel could be released and escape punishment, but he was unable to do so (vs. 14). By sundown, it became clear that the king could not deliver Daniel. God's prophet would have to be given to the lions.

The Result

We can get some idea of where the lions' den would have been located in ancient Babylon. The famous royal hanging gardens of Babylon were considered to be one of the seven wonders of the ancient world. The story behind their origin is that Nebuchadnezzar married a wife from the mountainous country of Media. Coming down to the flat, dry, hot plain of Mesopotamia, she longed for the pleasant features of her mountain homeland. To lessen her home-sickness, Nebuchadnezzar built the renowned hanging gardens of Babylon. Recent studies have suggested that these gardens were lo-cated in the northwestern corner of the palace, adjacent to the Euphrates River.

In all likelihood the royal zoo was located beside the royal gar-dens. Thus the same water that was used to irrigate the gardens could be used to water the animals, and the gardens would provide a proper habitat for some of the animals in the zoo. Thus the lions' den into which Daniel was thrown probably was located in the northwestern corner of the palace area.

Reports arose prior to World War I that the lions' den from which Daniel was miraculously delivered had been located and excavated by archaeologists. Excavations were going forward at Babylon, and Christian pilgrims came back from these diggings with the report that the lions' den had been found. The source of these erroneous rumors was Robert Koldewey, the excavator of Babylon. Koldewey was an unbeliever and an irreverent man. He was also a practical joker. Pilgrims would arrive asking questions about things such as the lions' den. Without hesitation, Koldewey would take them to some part of his excavations and say, "This is exactly the spot where it happened."

The pilgrims went home rejoicing to have seen where Daniel suf-fered and was delivered. When one of Koldewey's associates argued with him about what he was doing to these gullible people, Koldewey replied, "Why should I take from them one of the great experiences of their trip?"

Although we haven't located the scene of Daniel's deliverance from the lions, the clay tablets upon which the Babylonians kept their records do shed light on his experience. From the city of Ur, farther south, have come records which tell about the supplies for the feed-ing of the lions. Just as bureaucrats recorded the foodstuffs distrib-uted to different officials, they also recorded the food that was distributed to animals in the royal zoo—including the lions. These texts come from the time of the Ur III Dynasty, or approximately 2000 B.C., the time of Abraham. Not only did Babylon have lions in the royal zoo in the time of Daniel in the middle of the first millennium B.C., the records show they already had them there as early as the beginning of the second millennium B.C.

Darius was upset. Although he had no choice but to throw Daniel into the lions' den, he didn't like it. He didn't like it because he had been tricked into it by his own officials. More than that, he was genuinely concerned for Daniel; he had a great affection and respect for him. The king could not sleep all that night (vs. 18). Darius already knew of Daniel's God, and he had some inkling that He could act on Daniel's behalf (vs. 16), but he was not yet a believer. He might have gotten a full night's sleep if he had had a little stronger faith in Daniel's God!

God did not desert Daniel in the lions' den any more than He had deserted Daniel's three friends in the furnace. As on the earlier occasion, He sent His angel to be with Daniel and to protect him. Daniel told the king on the following morning when he came to inquire about the prophet's welfare, "O king, live forever! My God sent his angel, and he shut the mouths of the lions. They have not hurt me, because I was found innocent in his sight. Nor have I ever done any wrong before you, O king" (vss. 21, 22). Daniel did not claim credit for his own deliverance. He acknowledged God's mighty angel who had done this for him. In answer to his prayers, God had granted Daniel divine protection. God may not always answer prayers in such a dramatic way, but we can be certain He hears us when we pray today as surely as He heard Daniel's prayers in the lions' den.

Does God still perform such miracles today? Or is Daniel's experience just a story from long ago and far away that has little to do with modern life as we live it? From Recife, Brazil, comes a story illustrating that God is still active and can do for modern believers what He did for Daniel so many centuries ago. A man, working in the Recife city zoo, came in contact with Seventh-day Adventists, began studying the Bible, and was eventually baptized. Following his baptism, he came to work the next Monday morning with his new-found faith shining on his face. "A wonderful thing happened to me this Saturday," he told his fellow workers. "I was baptized into the Seventh-day Adventist Church!"

One of those listening to his testimony was particularly cynical toward Christianity. He replied, "Well, if you are such a great Christian, why don't you jump down into this cage with the lions? Why don't you see if God will protect you?"

Immediately, without hesitation, this new Christian jumped down into the lions' cage! Now, I would not recommend doing that; there is such a thing as presumption rather than faith. But I also think the Holy Spirit honored this man's action as a testimony of his new-found faith.

As the man jumped into the cage, the movement attracted the attention of a large, male lion who came over to see what was happening. The lions in this cage, it should be noted, had not been fed for twenty-four hours. The large male lion came over to the man in his cage and sniffed his trousers. Then he turned around, went back to his place, lay down, and went to sleep! Perhaps God had sent His angel to deliver not only Daniel in times past, but this zookeeper in Recife, Brazil.

The purpose? Some time later, seven of his fellow zookeepers were baptized.

Daniel was delivered from the lions. But the effect was quite different when his enemies, who had plotted against him, were placed in the same den where Daniel had spent the night. The lions attacked them immediately (vs. 24), demonstrating how hungry they really were. Daniel says that one of the reasons God delivered him was because he was innocent (vs. 22). In plotting against Daniel, his enemies were also plotting against his God. As a result, they were judged guilty and punished accordingly. The *lex talionis*, the law of an eye for an eye and a tooth for a tooth, was operating here—not from any desire for revenge on Daniel's part, but by the will of Darius the Mede.

Although at this time the king was still probably a Zoroastrian by religious conviction, he could see the greatness and power of Daniel's God in this miraculous deliverance.

> Then King Darius wrote to all the peoples, nations and men of every language throughout the land: "May you prosper greatly! I issue a decree that in every part of my kingdom people

must fear and reverence the God of Daniel. For he is the living God and he endures forever; his kingdom will not be destroyed, his dominion will never end. He rescues and saves; he performs signs and wonders in the heavens and on the earth. He has rescued Daniel from the power of the lions" (vss. 25-27).

Because of Daniel's faithful witness, God's character became known throughout the kingdom of Babylon to a degree it had never been known before. When he knelt to pray in spite of the prohibition, Daniel probably never dreamed of the far-reaching effect such an apparently insignificant act would cause. He probably saw it merely as a part of his normal round of daily activities, unimportant in and of itself except that, through it, he came into contact with his God. Yet, through that act of prayer, in defiance of the law, the name and character of the true and living God became known throughout the kingdom.

In the same way, our little acts of kindness, faith, and love may also have an effect that reaches as far as eternity. Through the faithful witness of Daniel, God calls us to a similar life of faith.

Daniel 3 and 6 in Summary

These two chapters present similar pictures; in both, Hebrews are being persecuted by a foreign king. In the first case, the king was Nebuchadnezzar of Babylon, and in the second, it was Darius the Mede, a vassal king of Babylon under the Persian emperor Cyrus. Both kings utilized Hebrews in their civil service. In both cases, these Hebrews were faithful in their service to the king and also to their God. It was this latter quality—their faithfulness to God—that got them in trouble. Because of their dedication to God, Daniel's three friends were thrown into the fiery furnace. Because of his dedication to God, Daniel himself was cast into the den of lions. In both cases miraculous deliverances took place—from the furnace and from the lions' den. And in both instances the foreign king was convinced that divine intervention had taken place on behalf of these servants of the true God. Both kings proclaimed throughout the kingdom the power and majesty of the God of heaven.

In terms of themes, then, these two chapters relate events that share many similarities. Of course, these similarities were worked out in different ways. The two events probably took place more than fifty years apart. The nature and location of the trials were different, the king on the throne was different, the deliverances took place in different ways, and the words chosen by the monarchs with which to praise the God of heaven were different.

Nevertheless, the overarching concerns of both episodes were the same. In both, the saints of God were put on trial and were delivered from that trial through divine intervention. So, we can say that the similarities between these two events are major in scope, while their differences are matters of detail.

The chiastic literary structure to be found in Daniel's book, in which form complements function, also underlines the similarities between chapters 3 and 6. In this volume, we have already noted the chiastic structure of Daniel and the fact that in the Aramaic section of the book, the chapters are arranged in pairs (see page 46). Chapters 3 and 6 form one such pair describing persecutions suffered by the Hebrews in exile. Daniel intentionally arranged his writings in this way to show the interrelated nature of the chapters and the unity of his writing. Literary critics who attempt to divide these units and distribute them to different sources written at different times have missed the point of the writer who expresses the unity of his book in a very bold and aesthetic way.

■ Applying the Word

Daniel 3, 6

1. **If I had been present on the plain of Dura when the music began, would I have been faithful to my convictions? Or would I have bowed down thinking I could take it back later or say it didn't count? What experiences have I faced that called for taking a stand—and how did I react? What can such experiences teach me about greater tests to come?**

2. What does the faithfulness of Daniel and his friends teach me about faith under pressure? What do these chapters teach me about God's commitment to His people?
3. What relationship does my devotional life have to my ability to meet tests of my faith? How would I rate my present devotional life? In what ways is it adequate? In what ways is it inadequate? What specific steps can I take today to strengthen it?
4. Would I be willing to die for my faith? If so, why? If not, why not?

■ Researching the Word

1. Study the persecution of early Christians in the book of Acts in the light of Daniel 3 and 6. List the episodes of persecution in Acts and the ways that the early Christians responded to them. In what ways were the episodes in Acts similar to those in Daniel? In what ways were they different? Compared to Daniel and his friends, in what ways were the Christian's responses to persecution similar and different?
2. Compare the persecutions depicted in Revelation 12 and 13 with those in Daniel 3 and 6. What common elements do you find? What can we learn from the experience of Daniel and his friends that will help us in the predicted crisis yet to come?

■ Further Study of the Word

1. For more on the historical circumstances and background of Daniel 3, see W. H. Shea, "Daniel 3: Extra-Biblical texts and the Convocation on the Plain of Dura," 29-52.
2. For further study on the question of the identity of Darius the Mede, see W. H. Shea, "Darius the Mede: An Update," 229-248; W. H. Shea, "Darius the Mede in His Persian-Babylonian Setting," 235-257; F. D. Nichol, ed., *The SDA Bible Commentary*, vol. 4, 814-817; John C. Whitcomb, *Darius the Mede*.

3. On Babylon as it was when conquered by the Persian kings, see S. H. Horn, *The Spade Confirms the Book*, chapters 4 through 7.

CHAPTER FIVE

Fallen Kingdoms

Daniel 2, 7

Chapters 2 and 7 of Daniel deal with the same general subject—prophecies regarding the rise and fall of four major Mediterranean world powers. The first of these prophecies was given to a pagan king, Nebuchadnezzar, in a dream as he slept at night (2:1). The second was given to the prophet Daniel himself as he slept in his bed at night (7:1, 2). So although the mode of revelation was virtually the same in both instances, the recipients were quite different. This contrast clearly accounts for some of the differences in content between the two prophecies.

Even a cursory look makes it apparent that the dream given to Nebuchadnezzar was much more simple than the one given to Daniel. Nebuchadnezzar saw only a great image composed of four metals from top to bottom with its feet a mixture of clay and metal. Then a great stone struck the image on the feet, smashed it, and disposed of it. This stone then grew until it filled the whole world.

The interpretation is that the four metals represent four kingdoms, so the meaning is quite straightforward and direct. Four great Mediterranean world powers were to occupy the stage of history, one after the other. Then the fourth power would become mixed up with other elements. Finally, the kingdom of God would replace all earthly kingdoms, and in contrast to them, it would stand forever.

In Daniel 7, the message is given directly to God's prophet and thus to God's people. The outline of kingdoms remains the same but includes more details. In this prophecy, four beasts, or animals, represent the four world kingdoms. The four beasts that appear in chapter 7 correspond to the four

*metals found in the image of Daniel 2. But there is a much greater oppor-
tunity to express details in the second prophecy because animals are ani-
mate, whereas metals are not. Thus the kingdoms that were outlined with
mere generalizations in Daniel 2 have their features fleshed out in Daniel
7. As the text progresses from revelation to a pagan king to the revelation
given to a prophet of God, it also progresses from a more general prophetic
outline to one that contains more details. This is a pattern that continues
throughout Daniel's book. Even more details are added in chapters 8 and
11.*

*This feature of Daniel's book brings up the subject of hermeneutics, or
rules of interpretation. There are two different schools of thought about
how the prophecies of Daniel should be approached.*

*In one case, critical scholars advance the theory that the proper method is
to start with chapter 11 and work backward through chapters 8, 7, and 2.
Thus Daniel 11 becomes the yardstick by which to approach the other prophecies of Daniel's book. These scholars feel that most of Daniel 11 deals with
the Greek king Antiochus Epiphanes, who ruled the Seleucid kingdom from
Antioch to Syria from approximately 175 B.C. to 164 B.C. Having deter-
mined that he is the main subject of the prophecies in Daniel 11, these
critical scholars then read him back into the other prophecies of Daniel's
book. Thus, Antiochus Epiphanes comes to be the all-encompassing figure
of Daniel's prophecies.*

*The other approach starts with Daniel 2 and works progressively through-
out the successive outline prophecies of the book—chapters 7, 8, and 11.
This approach results in a very different view of Daniel's prophecies. In
this approach, the succession of world kingdoms is clearly Babylon, Medo-
Persia, Greece, and Rome. Under the first scheme, Antiochus Epiphanes
becomes the major figure of Daniel's prophecies throughout the book.
Under the second, Antiochus Epiphanes is scaled down to a very modest
subheading under the Greek kingdom.*

Which of these two approaches is correct?

*The development we have already noted between Daniel 2 and 7 points
the way to the method inherent in the biblical text itself. Since Daniel 2 is
the more simple prophecy and Daniel 7 adds detail and is the more complex, it seems natural and logical to begin with the more simple prophecy
and work on through the book to the more complex, adding the details*

presented by each successive prophecy.

In either system it is clear that the book contains four main outline prophecies, chapters 2 and 7 in the Aramaic portion of the book and chapters 8 and 11 in the portions written in Hebrew. (The prophecy of chapter 9 is of a somewhat different nature since it concentrates on the future of the Jewish people and their Messiah, instead of viewing the nations of the world around them.) These four major outline prophecies are connected like a series of parallel electrical circuits. All four go over the same ground, but they progressively fill in more and more details. This parallelism is evident from the language used in the prophecies, the symbols found in them, and the interpretation given to them in the book itself.

Chapter 2, the first of these four outline prophecies, has the longest introduction. It recounts the circumstances under which this prophecy was given and how it was interpreted. In contrast, the prophecy in chapter 7 has a very short introduction consisting of a dateline and Daniel's statement that the prophecy came to him directly in a dream. The longer historical introduction to the prophecy of chapter 2 serves as a transition to connect the history of Daniel's book with the prophecies to be found in it. In chapter 2, in what is still commonly known as the historical section of Daniel, we find a significant transition from history to prophecy.

■ Getting Into the Word

Daniel 2

Read Daniel 2 through carefully at least two times. On the second reading, begin to deal with the following items:

1. **In your Daniel notebook, outline the events that lead up to the first mention of Daniel in verse 13. What brought Daniel onto the scene of action? Why was he successful when the other wise men were not able to tell the king his dream or to interpret it? What explanation does Daniel give for his ability?**
2. **In your Daniel notebook, list the basic symbols of Nebuchadnezzar's dream as reported in verses 31-36. Then,**

in a parallel column, list the interpretation of each of those symbols as explained in verses 36-45.

3. According to the message Daniel gave to the king, what was the dream's general meaning? How much of this dream do you think Nebuchadnezzar understood? What would have been the most meaningful part of the dream to him? What relationship, if any, do you see between Daniel 2:38, 39 and Daniel 3:1-6? What was the king seeking to prove in chapter 3?

4. At what point during Nebuchadnezzar's reign did he receive this prophetic dream? Why do you think God sent it at that time? Could it have been more effective in his experience if it had been given to him later in his reign? What would have been happening then? Review the lessons learned in Daniel 3 and 4. What do other chapters in Daniel tell us about Nebuchadnezzar's later experiences? How do they relate to this episode? What progression do you see?

5. How far into the future do you think a prophet of God can see? How far from his own time did Daniel see through Nebuchadnezzar's dream and through the parallel prophecies given directly to him? What does Daniel 2 tell us about God? What does it tell us about divine foreknowledge?

6. As you understand the message of the dream, in what part of it are you now living? What is to come next?

■ Exploring the Word

The Setting

Daniel had not been in Babylon long before his life was threatened! The threat grew out of an event that occurred by the second year of King Nebuchadnezzar's reign (2:1) which was either Daniel's second or third year in Babylon (the Babylonians did not number the year that the new king came to the throne as one of his regnal years). This threat was aimed not just at Daniel, but also at his friends, Shadrach, Meshach, and Abednego—and indeed, at the whole class of wise men in Babylon. By belonging to that class, Daniel and his friends found their lives endangered.

The danger arose from a dream the king had. Nebuchadnezzar did not understand the dream. In fact, when he woke up, he couldn't even remember what he had dreamed. However, he was impressed that it was very important. So he requested that his wise men help him. He summoned them and commanded them to tell him the dream and its interpretation. The wise men were quite willing to work on the interpretation but told the king he must first tell them the contents of the dream. The king tried every class of wise men available. "So the king summoned the magicians, enchanters, sorcerers and astrologers to tell him what he had dreamed" (vs. 2).

But each of these classes of wise men needed something to work with. The astrologers used the stars; the diviners used sheep livers; others used different signs in nature that signaled something to them—such as the birth of an animal with a congenital deformity. Nebuchadnezzar supplied none of these things. He had had a dream—an impressive dream—that now he could not remember. His wise men must supply the dream and its interpretation.

The king and his wise men were at loggerheads. The wise men said, "Tell your servants the dream, and we will interpret it" (vs. 4). The king responded, "So tell me the dream and interpret it for me" (vs. 6). Of course, the king was the only one with the power and authority to solve the impasse. The wise men merely served in an advisory capacity. The king was not pleased. He could see that his wise men's pretended ability to tell the future was dubious at best and they were stalling for time.

Again he demanded, "Tell me the dream, and I will know that you can interpret it for me" (vs. 9). The heat of the dialogue escalated—along with the king's anger. He had the last word. He pronounced a death decree upon all the wise men of the kingdom. If they were so worthless that they could not do what he asked of them, something supposedly well within their powers, he would do away with them all (vss. 12, 13).

Daniel and his three friends were not involved in this dialogue, but they did belong to the class of government workers that had been condemned. When news of the king's decree reached them through Arioch, commander of the king's guard, Daniel went in to the king to ask for more time so that he could attempt to present the dream and its interpretation to the king (vss. 14-16). Nebuchadnezzar had just accused the other wise men of trying to buy time (vs. 8), so one could imagine Daniel's request did not fall upon very welcoming ears. Nevertheless, since Daniel had not been party to the initial discussions, Nebuchadnezzar permitted him more time. Daniel came back with the answer the next day.

To achieve that goal, Daniel went into a prayer meeting with his friends (vss. 17, 18). Have you ever entered into prayer when your life counted on it? If Daniel did not come up with the contents of the king's dream, he would be killed—along with his friends and all the wise men of Babylon. A lot of people were counting on Daniel as he knelt to pray with his friends! One can only imagine the earnestness of the prayer.

And God answered! He had not forsaken or abandoned Daniel and his friends. They were still precious in His sight; He was looking out for them and protecting them. "During the night the mystery was revealed to Daniel in a vision" (vs. 19). At this point in the story, the text does not reveal the content of the dream to the reader. That comes later when Daniel reports to Nebuchadnezzar.

The story does recount, at this point, the song of joy that the Hebrews sang when they received the answer from God that would deliver them and the other wise men of Babylon. Their praise to God comes in the form of a brief psalm, or song—a piece of poetry (vss. 20-23). Not only is it a beautiful piece of poetry, it also expresses some of the key theological concepts of the history and prophecy that follow in the book of Daniel:

> Praise be to the name of God for ever and ever;
>   wisdom and power are his.
> He changes times and seasons;
>   he sets up kings and deposes them.
> He gives wisdom to the wise
>   and knowledge to the discerning.

He reveals deep and hidden things;
>   he knows what lies in darkness,
>   and light dwells with him.
I thank and praise you, O God of my fathers:
>   You have given me wisdom and power,
you have made known to me what we asked of you,
>   you have made known to us the dream of the king.

According to this brief poem, God is not an absentee landlord. He is present and active in the world and takes an active role in the nations. He can set up kings or he can depose them (vs. 21). To the unaided human eye, human history may appear to be a chaotic interplay of forces and counterforces. But Daniel assures us that behind all of this stands God, looking down upon it and moving within it to achieve what He sees best. At present, we may not understand all of these movements, but we can rest in the assurance of Daniel's words that God is truly active in the affairs of men and that He is working them out to His own best ends.

In addition, God makes known at times what will occur ahead in all this seemingly random play of world events. He gives this knowledge to His servants—not the wise men of Babylon, but prophets such as Daniel. God heard the prayer of Daniel and his friends for knowledge, and He gave "wisdom to the wise" (vs. 21).

God may not speak to us in visions and dreams today, but those who are sufficiently wise to seek Him will receive additional wisdom about the course they are to pursue and the course that history will follow. The light that dwells with God is sufficiently powerful to illuminate even the dark corners of history and the future of nations (vs. 22). The poem opens with a statement that wisdom and power belong to God (vs. 20); it ends with God providing wisdom and power to Daniel and his friends, revealing the king's dream to them (vs. 23).

When Daniel appeared before the king, Nebuchadnezzar asked him what he had asked the other wise men earlier: "Are you able to tell me what I saw in my dream and interpret it?" (vs. 26). The wise men had protested that the king's demand was not reasonable, that no man could perform what he asked of them (vs. 20). Daniel agreed that no human could tell the king what he had dreamed. In fact, he made it even more emphatic and specific. "No wise man, enchanter, magician or diviner can explain to the king the mystery he has asked about," declared Daniel (vs. 27). But what the wise men of Babylon and their gods were unable to accomplish, Daniel's God could do easily. "There is a God in heaven who reveals mysteries. He has shown King Nebuchadnezzar what will happen in days to come. Your dream and the visions that passed through your mind as you lay on your bed are these" (vs. 28). There is only one true God in heaven in contrast to the various gods of Babylon. This God reveals mysteries; He does not keep them hidden. He revealed the dream to Daniel to give to the king (vs. 28).

The Dream

If Daniel got the dream wrong, it could have cost him his life. But he did not get the dream wrong, because he received it from God, and God was the one who had given it to Nebuchadnezzar in the first place. God had spoken to the king in a dream, and now He was using His servant Daniel to make His message even more plain and clear to Nebuchadnezzar.

As explained by Daniel to the king, the dream consisted primarily of one great object—an image. The word used for *image* is the word commonly used in the Old Testament for an image, or idol. It is the word also used in Daniel 3 for the great image the king later erected on the plain of Dura. So the concept of an image would not have been unfamiliar to Nebuchadnezzar. Normally, however, the images of the gods with which he was acquainted were covered with a single type of metal—either gold or silver foil—or possibly cast in bronze. What was distinctive about the image Nebuchadnezzar saw in his dream was that it consisted of a series of metals, not just one. Nebuchadnezzar's response to this can be seen in Daniel 3. He built his own image to correspond to the one that he had seen in his dream, with one difference—his image was all of gold. This expressed his reaction against the image he had seen in his dream.

The metals in the image of Nebuchadnezzar's dream decreased in value but increased in strength. Moving from the golden head, through the silver and bronze, to the iron at the bottom, there was an ascending scale of strength and a descending scale of value. The feet of the image were its most curious part; the iron continued, but mixed with clay (2:33), obviously a poor choice of material for attempting to hold the iron pieces in place.

One final scene in the vision introduced another element—the rock (vss. 34, 35). It was an unusual rock in that it was cut out, or quarried, but not by human hands. No chisel marks of the stone masons defaced it. It was not part of the image. Instead, it struck the image like a ballistic missile hurled from the outside, causing the image to shatter and crumble into pieces. The rock was stronger than all the metals that had been used in the image—even the strongest of them, the iron in the legs. Nothing could withstand this rock.

The Interpretation

Nebuchadnezzar was satisfied that Daniel had told him the correct dream, the one he had previously had but could not remember. In this, Daniel surpassed the ability of all the wise men of Babylon. He did not attribute this to his own intelligence or skill. He freely pointed to the wisdom, power, and knowledge of the God he served. God had revealed the dream to Daniel (vss. 28, 47). His confidence that Daniel had related the dream correctly now gave Nebuchadnezzar confidence that Daniel could also interpret it correctly.

Daniel began his explanation of the image starting from the top. "Contrary to what you would normally expect, O King, this is not an image of a god. It is, rather, a symbol that stands for something else. And you are part of it. You are the head of gold" (see verses 37, 38). Clearly, Daniel was not talking just about Nebuchadnezzar; he was referring as well to the empire that Nebuchadnezzar had built. This becomes clear when Daniel comes to the second metal in the image, representing the next world kingdom. "After you, another kingdom will rise, inferior to yours. Next, a third kingdom" (vss. 39,

40). Thus we are dealing here with kingdoms, not just kings. Still, it was appropriate to identify the Neo-Babylonian kingdom with Nebuchadnezzar. He was the one who had built this empire militarily; he was the one who had vastly expanded the city of Babylon architecturally; and he ruled that empire forty-three of the sixty-six years it existed. The direct connection of Nebuchadnezzar with the Neo-Babylonian Empire was quite fitting and appropriate (see map of the Babylonian Empire on page 141).

Following Nebuchadnezzar's Babylon, another kingdom would arise that would be inferior to Babylon. Extrabiblical history and the books of Daniel, Ezra, and Nehemiah tell us that Medo-Persia followed Babylon (see map of the Persian Empire on page 147). In this volume, we have already looked at Daniel 5 and 6, which recount the Persian conquest of Babylon and how the Persians set up their government in the former Babylonian territory. We saw there, too, how Daniel referred obliquely and symbolically to the transition from Babylon to Medo-Persia when he described "the gods of silver and gold, of bronze, iron, wood and stone" (5:23), reversing the order found here in chapter 2 and placing the silver before the gold on the very night that the silver kingdom of the Persians took over from the golden kingdom of Babylon.

Historically, in what sense was the Persian kingdom inferior to that of Nebuchadnezzar? After all, the Persians conquered Babylon, and Medo-Persia actually came to include more territory than the Babylonian Empire. But superiority can exist in other areas besides mere square miles.

The culture of Babylon was renowned throughout the ancient world, while that of the Medes and Persians was looked down upon as rustic and primitive. The Persians had no written language until the time of their empire. Old Persian was created as a written language by the Persian kings to use in inscribing monuments. They more commonly used the Elamite language for keeping their own records. On the other hand, the written Babylonian language went well back into the third millennium B.C., and that rich heritage of language brought with it all of the science, religion, and culture of the Babylonian Empire. So there were various ways in which Babylon

THE RISE OF THE NEO-BABYLONIAN EMPIRE

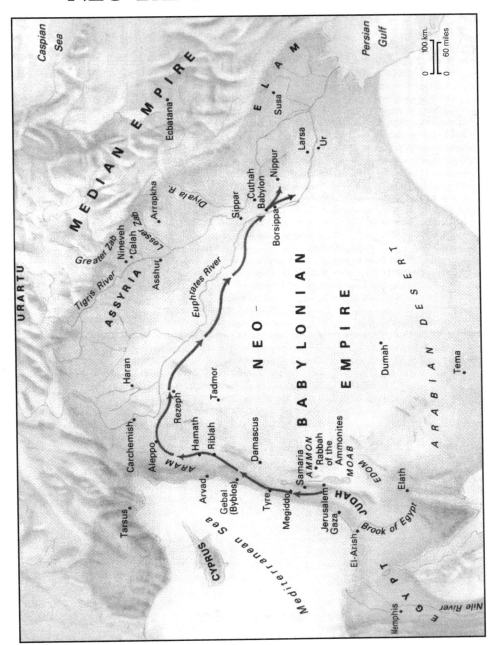

was superior to Persia, even though the Babylonians did not conquer as much territory as the Persians did.

The third kingdom depicted by the image was symbolized by bronze (2:39). The Greeks followed the Persians (see map of the Greek Empire on page 153). Although earlier commercial and cultural contacts had taken place, the great intrusion of Hellenism (Greek thought and culture) into the Near East came with the invasions of Alexander the Great. Not only did he defeat Darius III, the last Persian king, but he also marched all the way to the Indus Valley of northwestern India in his wide-ranging conquests. Alexander's kingdom did not last as long as either that of the Babylonians or the Persians, however, for after his death it soon splintered into a number of pieces which were taken over by the generals who had served under him.

These pieces of the Greek Empire were picked up by Rome and absorbed into that empire. The process took a century and a quarter—from the time Rome defeated mainland Greece in the early second century B.C. until Julius Caesar conquered Egypt in the late first century B.C. By that time, the Greek Empire had disappeared, having been absorbed by the next power on the scene of action, the iron kingdom of Rome (see map of the Roman Empire on page 159). With this conquest, the four main metal symbols of the image were complete. Thus, in historical order, the gold represents Babylon; the silver represents Medo-Persia; the bronze represents Greece; and the iron represents Rome.

What comes next? Are these all of the great Mediterranean world powers to come on the scene of action? Will there be other kingdoms greater than Rome? The prophecy takes an interesting turn at this point, for there are no more metals. There is, however, another element in the image; the symbol of clay (vs. 33). The iron continues, indicating that what follows after Rome will be Rome-like, but it will not be solid like Rome. It will be divided. These divisions are accentuated by the mixture of iron and clay. This is not the right way to build a strong image. To build a strong image, another metal should have been used, or more iron should have been added to the image. That was not the case. Instead, the weakening element of clay was added to the iron, thus taking away its strength.

The mixture of iron and clay represented the divisions and disunity that came to the Roman Empire:

> So this will be a divided kingdom; . . . As the toes were partly iron and partly clay, so this kingdom will be partly strong and partly brittle. And just as you saw the iron mixed with baked clay, so the people will be a mixture and will not remain united, any more than iron mixes with clay (vss. 41-43).

The emphasis here is upon disunion and disunity—a stark contrast with the iron that went before it. Iron was the hardest and most unified metal known to the ancient and classical worlds. From the strongest and most unified nation, the territory that had made up the Roman Empire would go to being the weakest and most divided. Such was the fate of Rome as described by the prophecy.

Historically, did the predicted disunity and mixing take place?

It is easy to see what happened to the Roman Empire under the onslaught of barbarian tribes. Under their impact, the city of Rome itself fell in A.D. 476. From that time forward, the Italian peninsula came under the control of the Ostrogoths for the better part of a century until their final defeat in A.D. 555. Historians commonly use the sixth century A.D. to mark the transition from Imperial Rome to Medieval Rome. When Rome entered that century, it was still powerful militarily and politically; it was a populous and prosperous city that was still beautiful in its architecture and monuments. When Rome came out of that century, it was a broken-down, depopulated center that controlled virtually nothing. The clay had been introduced into the iron.

This state of affairs was to continue until the end (vss. 33-35). In spite of the military conquerors of the past and the political leagues of the present, the nations of Europe (not to mention the rest of the Roman Empire) have not cleaved one to the other. Will the European Common Market and the political affiliation of European countries negate this picture? They may, with difficulty, agree upon certain political principles, and they may enter into agreements to facilitate trade and commerce, but each of these countries may be expected to retain control of its cultural, linguistic, and territorial properties. They may join together for certain common purposes, but according to Daniel's prophecy, they will never be joined into one complete political entity as was the Roman Empire.

It is interesting to see how the events tearing at the fabric of Roman society looked to a contemporary commentator on prophecy. The church father, Jerome, lived through the late fourth century and the early fifth century A.D., so he saw some of the breakup of the Roman Empire taking place. His commentary on Daniel was dedicated in the year 407. As he read through the prophecy of Daniel 2, he saw these events taking place before his very eyes. Even though the worst was yet to come, he still could write:

> Moreover the fourth kingdom, which plainly pertains to the Romans, is the iron which breaks in pieces and subdues all things. But its feet and toes are partly of iron and partly of clay, which at this time is most plainly attested. For just as in its beginning nothing was stronger and more unyielding than the Roman Empire, so at the end of its affairs nothing is weaker. (*Commentary on Daniel*, comments on 2:40, column 504).

This is not the end of the vision, however, for there is one more stage in the image's career—its destruction and the scattering of its fragments to the four winds. In symbol this is accomplished by the great stone which strikes the image on the feet of iron and clay. It smashed them, and

> then the iron, the clay, the bronze, the silver and the gold were broken to pieces at the same time and became like chaff on a threshing floor in the summer. The wind swept them away without leaving a trace. But the rock that struck the statue became a huge mountain and filled the whole earth (vs. 35).

In other words, all the kingdoms of this world will eventually be destroyed and swept away, and there will be no further human kingdoms to succeed them. The kingdom that would follow would be of an entirely different nature, represented not by a metal, but by a rock cut out without human hands (vs. 34). It was to be a kingdom of an entirely different order from those preceding it. According to Daniel's divinely-inspired interpretation: "In the time of those kings, the God of heaven will set up a kingdom that will never be destroyed, nor will it be left to another people. It will crush all those kingdoms and bring them to an end, but it will itself endure forever" (2:44).

This is the central fact of the conclusion to this dream-vision: that the God of heaven will one day set up a kingdom that will never be destroyed. It will never be displaced by another metal kingdom that will come down the road of history, for history itself will end in that kingdom of God. It will be history's great climax. This is the goal toward which history is moving.

The Results

Several results occurred from Daniel's recitation before the king of the dream and its interpretation. First, there was a result for Nebuchadnezzar. He recognized that this was the very dream he had dreamed and that Daniel had recalled it correctly. This had a tremendous impact upon the king. Just as he would have fallen down to worship the image that he saw in the dream, he virtually fell down to worship Daniel who brought him a knowledge of the dream. "Then King Nebuchadnezzar fell prostrate before Daniel and paid him honor and ordered that an offering and incense be presented to him" (vs. 46). He recognized, however, the source of Daniel's wisdom did not come merely from Daniel's own intelligence. He realized it came from Daniel's God. His act of respectful recognition of Daniel took careful note of this distinction. "Surely," the king declared, "your God is a God of gods and the Lord of kings and a revealer of mysteries, for you were able to reveal this mystery" (vs. 47).

At this point in his experience, Nebuchadnezzar could still be classified as a polytheist, but he was moving, under the influence of Daniel and his true God, toward henotheism—a belief in the superiority of one god, without denying the existence of other gods.

THE PERSIAN EMPIRE

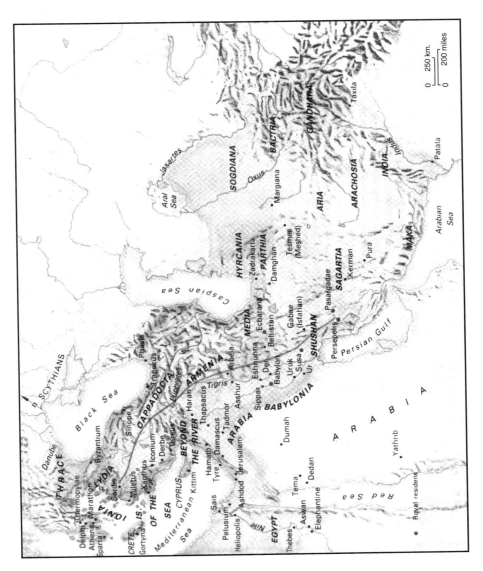

MEDIA Satrapy under Darius I
=== Canal built between the Gulf of Suez and the Nile
—— Royal Way

Nebuchadnezzar still recognized the existence of the gods of Babylon, but he acknowledged the superiority of Daniel's God, Yahweh. A knowledge of the true God of heaven was beginning to dawn upon his understanding. The picture was certainly not complete on this particular day, but Nebuchadnezzar had begun a spiritual journey that would not end until he finally came to an adequate knowledge of the true God as described in Daniel 4.

For Daniel and his friends, the dramatic turn of events in connection with the king's dream resulted in advancement up the ladder of the Babylonian bureaucracy. Nebuchadnezzar lavished gifts upon Daniel and made him ruler over the entire province of Babylon (vs. 48). He also placed Daniel in charge of all the wise men of Babylon. This seemed only fitting—especially since Daniel's success in interpreting the dream had just saved all their lives. Human nature being what it is, however, this probably did not endear Daniel to them. They remained at odds with him over a number of points. He had shown them up with his superior wisdom. Now he had authority over them, and he had carried out his search for wisdom in a way entirely different from their techniques. Daniel did not need to search sheep livers for anomalies or study the stars. He could pray directly to the true God who revealed deep mysteries to His servants. Undoubtedly, it didn't help relations between Daniel and the other wise men when Daniel requested—and secured—promotions for his three friends, Shadrach, Meshach, and Abednego, as administrators over the province of Babylon (vs. 49).

The king's dream and its interpretation not only had results for Nebuchadnezzar, Daniel, his friends, and the other Babylonian wise men. It continues to have implications for us some 2,500 years later.

How does it affect our lives today? It is a remarkable evidence of the foreknowledge of the true God. It demonstrates to us in a very real and concrete way—through the events of history—that there is a God in heaven and that He is concerned with human affairs. We can see His hand in history, and we can recognize His divine foreknowledge in this prophecy. We can actually check the interpretation to determine its accuracy. We can look back over the 2,500 years of history that have elapsed since Daniel's interpretation and see if those events really happened.

What of those, however, who believe that there is no supernatural element in Daniel's prophecies, that Daniel was simply thrown on his own resources in his attempt to give the king a plausible interpretation of his dream?

In evaluating such a possibility, we need to ask ourselves: If there is no supernatural source of information about the future, if Daniel simply had to hazard a human guess when he interpreted the king's dream, what kind of interpretation would he likely have given? What probable scenarios would have presented themselves to him?

First, he might well have tried to curry favor with Nebuchadnezzar. It would have been tempting to have told the king that the image was made entirely of gold and that it represented Babylon which would stand forever. But Daniel did not bring that popular message to the king. Instead, he told Nebuchadnezzar that his kingdom was going to be succeeded by another. If Daniel 3 is any indication, such a message was not popular with the king! Under other circumstances, Daniel's life might have been endangered for bringing such a message to the king.

Second, it would have been natural for Daniel, unaided by divine revelation, to have drawn on a picture of history that was popular in the ancient world—a picture of a history that was cyclical and that would continue without end. There would not be just four world kingdoms followed by an end to human history. Rather, there would be five kingdoms, six, seven, eight, etc. Since human beings had acted in a certain way in the past, they should continue to act that way in the future, leading to an endless sequence of kingdoms.

Daniel chose to neither curry favor with the king nor engage in historical philosophical speculations. He chose, instead, to declare that there would be exactly four world kingdoms that would follow each other in succession—not one, two, or three, but four. And the fourth would not signal an end to human history, but would disintegrate and be followed by another period of history marked by this divided condition. He predicted precisely four kingdoms followed by divisions that would not be put back together again. How did Daniel know that there would be exactly four kingdoms—Babylon, Medo-Persia, Greece, and Rome—followed by a divided condition representing the break-up of Imperial Rome?

How did Daniel know this? He tells us. "There is a God in heaven who reveals mysteries. He has shown . . . what will happen in days to come" (vs. 28). His wisdom is available to man, to His servants the prophets such as Daniel. Through Daniel, it has been revealed to us. As we meet the 2,500-year-old word of Daniel, we meet the word of the living God today. He cared enough to speak this truth to one individual, Nebuchadnezzar, and He still cares enough to speak that truth to each of us today.

One final point regarding this dream and its interpretation should concern us: Where in the course of history, as outlined by this symbolic dream, do we live? We do not live back in the time of Babylon and Medo-Persia with Daniel. We do not live in the time of the Roman Empire. We live at the very bottom of the image, in the divided times of the feet and toes.

What happened next in Nebuchadnezzar's dream? The stone struck the image, smashing it to pieces, which the wind blew away. The stone then became a great mountain and filled the whole earth (vss. 34, 35). That means the God of heaven is going to set up His kingdom soon. We can prepare to enter it by giving our hearts to the same God who provided divine wisdom to Daniel. We can praise Him and honor Him and glorify Him in the same way that Daniel did. When we do, we will be prepared to enter into that same kingdom with Daniel. There, with him, we can cast our crowns of salvation before the Lord and praise Him for His glorious love to us.

■ Getting Into the Word

Daniel 7

Read Daniel 7 through at least two times. Then work through the following questions and exercises:

1. **Divide a page in your Daniel notebook into three columns. In the first column, list the basic symbols and kingdoms Daniel sees in verses 2-14. In the second column, place the**

equivalent symbols and kingdoms from the prophecy of Daniel 2. In the third column, specify, as far as possible, the historical kingdoms and events symbolized by each stage of the parallel prophecies of Daniel 2 and 7.

2. Develop a list of characteristics for each of the beast powers in Daniel 7. Do the same for the little horn power. Utilize all of chapter 7 for this exercise. In what ways do the additional details given in Daniel 7 illuminate the history of the kingdoms first presented in Daniel 2?

3. How does Daniel 2 reach its climax and conclusion? How does Daniel 7 reach its climax and conclusion? What are the similarities? What are the differences? What additional details does Daniel 7 add to the final climax?

4. Is Christ portrayed directly in the prophecy of Daniel 2? Is Christ portrayed directly in the prophecy of Daniel 7? How is Christ portrayed in the prophecy of Daniel 7? What reasons can you give for the differences?

5. How is your understanding of God's foreknowledge affected by the prophecies in these two chapters? How is your impression of God as a personal God affected by these two prophecies?

■ Exploring the Word

The Setting

Daniel 2 begins with a long historical recital of the circumstances under which the dream-vision of Daniel 2 was first given and then recovered and interpreted. It tells of the experience of Nebuchadnezzar, Daniel, and the wise men at court in Babylon in the sixth century B.C. In that sense, chapter 2 stems from a historical experience and recites that experience to us. At least half of chapter 2 is historical narrative; the remainder is prophecy.

Daniel 7 is different. It gives only a simple, short historical setting (vs. 1). It tells us little more of the local, contemporary historical setting than the date (Belshazzar's first year) and where Daniel

THE EMPIRE OF
ALEXANDER THE GREAT

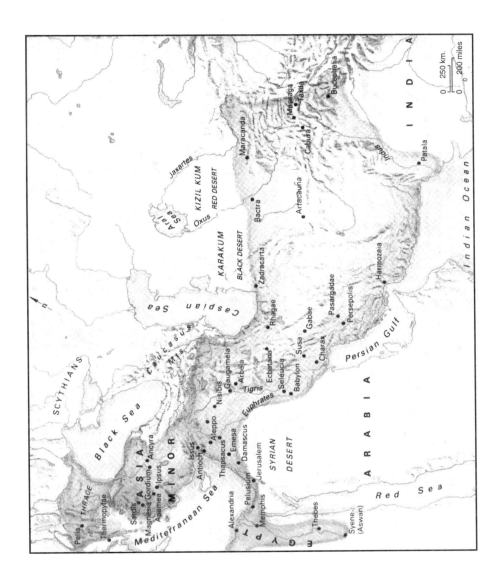

was when he received this vision. With that minor exception, Daniel 7 is directly and completely prophetic throughout. Daniel 2 is approximately half history and half prophecy; Daniel 7 is nearly all prophecy. In this, it sets the tone for the rest of Daniel, which is all prophecy.

When we compare the way the prophecy of chapter 7 was given with that of chapter 2, we find both similarities and differences. Both Nebuchadnezzar (chap. 2) and Daniel (chap. 7) were asleep on their beds when they received their respective visions. Thus the mode of revelation in these two cases was the same. The recipients, however, were quite different. The dream of chapter 2 was given to a pagan king initially for his own personal benefit; the dream of Daniel 7 was given directly to the prophet Daniel to communicate to God's people.

The different recipients also emphasize the different roles Daniel played in these two experiences. In chapter 2, he eventually received the vision and its interpretation from God, but his function was primarily that of an inspired wise man to explain the dream to the king. In chapter 7, Daniel received the dream directly from God. *Chronologically*, this is the first such occurrence in the book of Daniel. (Remember that the chapters as they presently appear in Daniel are not arranged in chronological order.) So the vision of chapter 7 actually constitutes Daniel's call to the office of prophet in his own right, being the first time he received a vision directly from God.

The Dream

The vision of Daniel's dream began with a view of "the great sea" (vs. 2). Winds were blowing upon the sea, churning it into an agitated state. Daniel saw four beasts come up out of the sea, one after another (vs. 3). Geographically, this great sea can be identified with the Mediterranean because each of the four nations which Daniel saw portrayed were Mediterranean world powers—either located in the Mediterranean area or conquering territory to its shores.

The successive visions of Daniel's book show a progression in the degree of activity they involve. In Daniel 2, the great image just stood there. Here in Daniel 7, the beasts Daniel saw emerge from the water demonstrate different characteristics, but their actions still are not directed toward a specific goal. In Daniel 8, the actions of the ram and the goat, become directional. The ram charges west, and the goat charges east toward the ram and challenges it. This directional activity is not yet developed in the vision of Daniel 7, however, and we need to rely for understanding more upon the characteristics the animals manifest than those they act out.

As Daniel describes the vision of chapter 7, he says the first beast he saw emerging from the sea looked to him "like a lion" (vs. 4). It was an animal he could recognize, but at the same time, it was not a completely normal lion, because it had wings on its back. Daniel watched as those wings were plucked off. It stood up on its two hind feet like a man, and a man's heart was given to it (vs. 4). The interpretation given by the angel later in the chapter does not identify this beast-nation by name.

The second beast to come up out of the waters was a bear (vs. 5). This bear was somewhat disfigured, being raised up higher on one side than the other. It had three ribs in its mouth, representing its conquests. The bear is an animal which lives in the mountains, suggesting that the kingdom represented by this animal would come from a mountainous region.

The third beast to appear was a leopard. While it had something of the normal configuration of a leopard, it also had some unusual features. Instead of having one head, it had four. Like the lion, it also had wings on its back—four of them to match the number of its heads (vs. 6).

The fourth beast Daniel saw was not like any of the others nor like anything he had seen before. It appears to have been a composite beast made up of various features of different animals. It also appears to have been the most fierce of the four and was definitely a conquering, crushing power as it took up its activities (vs. 7).

One of the strange characteristics of this fourth beast was the fact that it had ten horns. As the vision unfolded, Daniel observed a great deal of activity going on among these horns. First, a little horn, smaller than the others, started to grow up among the ten. Although it began small, it soon became bigger than the others. As it grew and became stronger, this little horn uprooted three of the other horns (vss. 7, 8). Its activities were described in distinctly religious terms. It uttered blasphemy, and it persecuted the saints (vs. 25).

As Daniel continued to look, his view was directed to heaven where he was shown a great heavenly tribunal. The heavenly court convened and passed sentence upon the beast, the little horn, and all mankind (vss. 9, 10). Following the execution of the sentence against the beast, Daniel saw God set up His everlasting kingdom. The saints of the Most High were ushered into His kingdom, where the Son of Man would rule over them forever and ever. Through the ages, God's saints have been under the authority of the different world powers as they have emerged one after the other. But the ultimate destiny of the saints is to live in God's eternal kingdom under the wise, benevolent rulership of God and His Son (vss. 13, 14).

The Interpretation

In his vision, Daniel turned to an angel standing nearby and asked him the meaning of these things (vss. 15, 16). In response, the angel gave him a brief explanation, saying "the four great beasts are four kingdoms which will rise from the earth. But the saints of the Most High will receive the kingdom and will possess it forever—yes, for ever and ever" (vs. 18). Beyond the travail of this earth's history lies God's kingdom, the ultimate answer to all of the problems created by those earthly kingdoms.

After more questioning from Daniel (vss. 19-22), the angel interpreter went on to give the prophet a longer explanation (vss. 23-27).

Identifying the Beasts.

In neither his brief answer nor the more detailed explanation did the angel interpreter name any of the kingdoms represented by the four beasts. How, then, are we to identify them? We can do so by comparing them with the other prophecies of Daniel. A comparison with Daniel 2 provides the name of the kingdom with which this sequence begins. A comparison with Daniel 8 gives us the names of two more powers in the succession of kingdoms.

Are such comparisons legitimate? Can we be certain, for example, that chapter 2 and chapter 7 are describing the same four kingdoms? We know that the sequence in chapter 2 began with Babylon (2:38, 39) because Daniel plainly told Nebuchadnezzar so. If chapter 7 is describing the same sequence of kingdoms, then the first symbol in that chapter must likewise represent Babylon. The question, then, becomes: What evidence do we find that chapters 2 and 7 are dealing with the same broad prophetic outline?

The first link occurs on the broadest scale—literary structure. In the chiastic literary structure of the first half of Daniel's book, chapters 2 and 7 are found in corresponding, parallel locations (see the discussion of Daniel's literary structure on pages 44-47). Just as common themes link chapter 4 with chapter 5, and chapter 3 with chapter 6, so also chapter 2 is linked with chapter 7 in terms of similar content. This means that they cover the same ground and should be seen as explanatory of each other.

The second link between these two prophecies is that both contain the same number of major elements. Daniel 2 brings to view a series of four kingdoms represented by four metals; chapter 7 depicts four major kingdoms under the symbolism of beasts emerging from the sea. Chapter 2 has the fourth kingdom divided by an intermingling of clay with the iron; in chapter 7, the division of the fourth kingdom is represented by the horns on that beast and the activity going on among them. In chapter 2, the series of four kingdoms is superseded by something entirely different—a stone kingdom that lasts forever; in chapter 7, the series of powers concludes with God's eternal kingdom, which the saints of the Most High will possess forever. Thus chapters 2 and 7 contain the same major elements even though they are given in different forms. Given the fact that these two chapters have similar outlines, it seems clear that the two prophecies are talking about the same kingdoms—with added enrichment in the latter chapter.

Beyond the similarity of general outline, there is specific language in these two chapters that tell us they are dealing with the same number and sequence of kingdoms. In Daniel 2 the bronze kingdom is specifically enumerated as the "third" kingdom (vs. 39), and

THE ROMAN EMPIRE,
1ST CENTURY B.C. TO A.D. 150

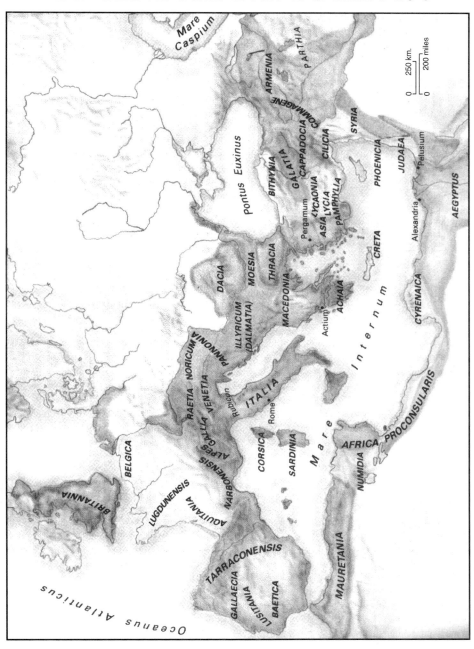

the iron kingdom is called the "fourth" kingdom (vs. 40). In Daniel 7, the "first," "second," and "fourth" beasts are identified with those specific numbers, and in the angel's interpretation, he says that the "four great beasts are four kingdoms" that will arise from the earth (vs. 17). Daniel gives us the numbers, and the angel gives us the interpretation of those numbers. The numbers are the same as those found in Daniel 2. Since both prophecies talk about exactly the same number of kingdoms, the implication is clear that they must be referring to the same powers.

As if to cement this relationship, the fourth kingdom in both visions was represented by iron—the image's iron legs of chapter 2 and the iron teeth of the fourth beast in chapter 7. Of the four animals found in chapter 7, the fourth beast alone contained iron, thus linking it directly with the fourth kingdom in Daniel 2.

Once we know that these two prophecies are talking about the same four kingdoms, it is easy to identify the lion, the first power depicted in the prophecy of chapter 7, as Babylon—since Daniel specifically identifies the first kingdom in chapter 2:38, 39 with that power. The sequence of the succeeding three beasts in chapter 7 should, therefore, be identified with the same kingdoms that we have described in the interpretation of chapter 2—Medo-Persia, Greece, and Rome.

The beasts of chapter 7 can also be identified through the identifications given by name in Daniel 8. In this case, the second beast of Daniel 7 is parallel to the first beast of Daniel 8, and the third beast of Daniel 7 is parallel to the second beast of Daniel 8. How so?

The bear in Daniel 7 was lifted up on one side (vs. 5) while the ram in Daniel 8 had one of its horns standing up higher than the other (vs. 3). In 8:20, this ram is identified as Medo-Persia, and the dual nature of this kingdom is said to represent the two political entities out of which it was formed. Thus the bear of chapter 7 and the ram of chapter 8 represent the same power.

Likewise, the goat in chapter 8 with a "prominent horn between his eyes" (vs. 5) is identified as the power of Greece (vs. 21). This horn was uprooted, and four more horns came up in its place. This symbolism corresponds to the four heads and four wings on the leopard in chapter 7 so that the goat of chapter 8 and the leopard of chapter 7 represent the same powers.

We can diagram what we have learned thus:

Kingdom	Daniel 2	Daniel 7	Daniel 8	Identification
1	Gold	Lion	—	Babylon, 2:38, 39
2	Silver	Bear	Ram	Medo-Persia, 8:20
3	Bronze	Leopard	Goat	Greece, 8:21
4	Iron	Nondescript beast	King of fierce countenance	Rome

So, although the powers brought to view in chapter 7 are not named specifically, we can identify them with certainty as Babylon, Medo-Persia, Greece, and Rome through clear connections with the powers that *are* named specifically in chapters 2 and 8. It remains to identify their various characteristics and see how they fit into history.

The Babylonian lion (see map of the Babylonian Empire on page 141). The lion had wings on its back, giving it the rapidity of flight. This speed was demonstrated in Babylon's early conquests under Nebuchadnezzar. But Daniel watched as the wings were plucked off. The situation in Babylon changed; speed on the battlefield declined, and conquests grew scarce as the kingdom shrunk under weaker kings such as Nabonidus. No longer did Babylon have the heart of the conquering lion; it was reduced to the heart of a man with no more taste for conquest (7:4).

A lion was a particularly apt symbol to represent Babylon. Lions were depicted on the walls of Babylon's Ishtar gate and on the outer wall of the audience chamber of the king's palace. A statue of an immense lion stood in the courtyard of the palace. In the mythology of Babylon, these lions were thought of as carrying the goddess Ishtar on their backs.

The Persian bear (see map of the Persian Empire on page 147). We have already mentioned the twofold nature of the Medo-Persian kingdom as symbolized by the fact that the bear, the second power depicted in chapter 7, was raised up on one side (vs. 5). Through the ninth, eighth, and seventh centuries B.C., the kingdom of the Medes was a powerful force in the Near East, constantly threatening the dominant Assyrians. But in the sixth century B.C., the up-and-coming kingdom of Persia, under Cyrus, succeeded in conquering the Medes and fusing them into a combined Medo-Persian Empire. The three ribs in the mouth of the bear could easily represent the conquest of Lydia in Anatolia, or ancient Turkey, in 547 B.C, the conquest of Babylon in 539 B.C., and that of Egypt in 525 B.C. The first two conquests were accomplished by Cyrus after he had put the Medo-Persian Empire together; the campaign to Egypt was led by his son Cambyses.

The Greek leopard (see map of the Greek empire on page 153). The outstanding characteristic of the leopard was the wings on its back (vs 6). These wings denote speed, an apt illustration of the rapidity with which the Greeks conquered the Near East. It was all accomplished essentially in three short years by Alexander the Great. By comparison, it took the Assyrians three years (725–722 B.C.) to conquer Samaria and the Babylonians three years (589 B.C.– 586 B.C.) to conquer Jerusalem. Yet in the same amount of time Alexander conquered the whole of the ancient Near East, from Egypt to the Indus Valley of India!

But as rapid as this conquest was, it was not destined to last. The leopard's four heads (vs. 6) represented the four divisions into which Alexander's kingdom broke up after his death. His generals picked up the pieces of that kingdom and divided them into mainland Greece, Asia Minor, Syria (including Babylon), and Egypt (see map on page 165). This same historical division of the kingdom of Greece is represented by the four horns on the goat in Daniel 8:8, 22.

The Roman beast (see map of the Roman Empire on page 159). The fourth kingdom in chapter 7 represented Rome, which crushed and devoured its victims, trampling underfoot whatever remained (vs. 7). Archaeology has given us an excellent example of how apt a description this is of Rome's conquests. On the west side of Jerusalem, there used to be a valley known as the Tyropoean Valley, or "Cheesemaker's" Valley. It does not exist today because it was filled in with the debris of the Roman destruction of Jerusalem in A.D. 70.

The English archaeologist, Kathleen Kenyon, made a deep, narrow sounding into this area and found that the debris was some seventy feet deep! The Romans virtually swept the site of the old city of Jerusalem clean. Roman engineers were known for their thoroughness in both destruction and construction. In this way this power "crushed and devoured" (vs. 7).

Strong as it was, however, the Roman Empire was not to last either. By the fifth and sixth centuries A.D., Rome was crumbling under the assault of the barbarian tribes. The capital of the empire had moved to the east, to Constantinople, leaving a vacuum of leadership in the Italian peninsula. For a time, the Ostrogoths took over the region. In the middle of the sixth century A.D., however, the Ostrogoths were defeated and faded from history. When that happened, the leadership of the city and territory of Rome fell into the hands of the bishop of Rome. Much of his assumption of civil power dates to this time, when there was a vacuum of leadership in the region.

The Ten Horns and the Little Horn

These developments, connected, with the division and demise of the Roman Empire, are symbolized in the prophecy, first by the ten horns on the fourth beast, and then by the rise of the little horn. Of these ten horns the angel interpreter said, "The ten horns are ten kings who will come from this [fourth] kingdom" (vs. 24). The words for *king* and *kingdoms* are used rather interchangeably both in Daniel 7 and also in Daniel 2. In Daniel 7:17, where the NIV translates four "kingdoms," the original word is actually "kings." The same feature appears in chapter 2 where Daniel tells Nebuchadnezzar, "You, O *king*, are this head of gold," but, "after you shall arise another *kingdom* inferior to you" (vss. 38, 39, KJV, emphasis supplied). Thus the ten horns which protrude from the head of the Roman beast represent the different pieces into which the empire shattered under assault by the barbarian tribes then migrating into Europe and settling in various places (see map on page 171). The *coup de grace* of this process occurred in A.D. 476 when the city of Rome itself fell to the Heruli. These pagan tribes, represented by the ten

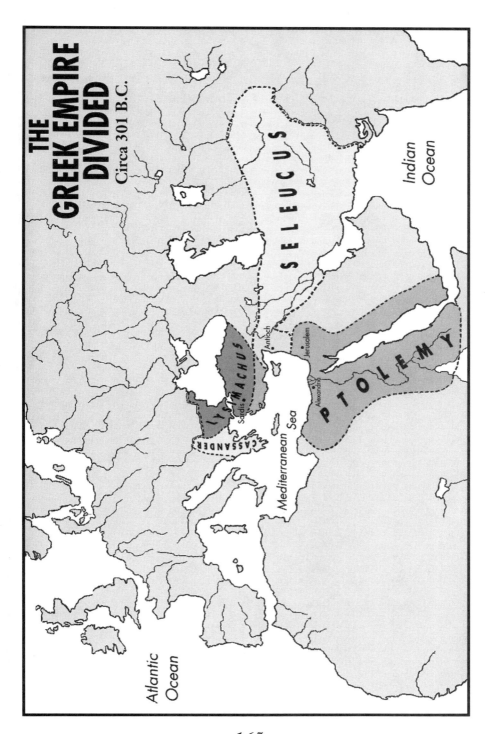

THE
**GREEK EMPIRE
DIVIDED**
Circa 301 B.C.

SELEUCUS

Indian
Ocean

LYSIMACHUS

CASSANDER

Antioch

Jerusalem

PTOLEMY

Sardis

Alexandria

Mediterranean Sea

Atlantic
Ocean

horns on the fourth beast, eventually developed into the modern nations of Europe. Considerable ingenuity has been exercised trying to identify precisely ten of these tribes-turned-nations. It probably is preferable to take the number ten as a round number which may have fluctuated up or down at any given historical time, according to the political and military fortunes of those various powers.

In Daniel's vision, he saw three of these horns plucked up before the rising power of the little horn (vs. 8). These three tribes can be identified with some degree of accuracy. As the various European tribes struggled for supremacy, the wars that were fought were both political and theological in nature, often combining territorial disputes with controverted points of religious doctrine. To a degree never before employed in Christianity, the power of the state came to be used to root out heretics. Justinian, the reigning Roman emperor in Constantinople, was happy to support the bishop of Rome in these struggles, both for his own political gain, and for the gain of the Roman-centered church. In A.D. 534, Justinian sent his army and navy against the Vandals in North Africa and defeated them.

Following that conquest, Belisarius, Justinian's general, led his troops on an invasion of the Italian peninsula to liberate the city of Rome from the Ostrogoths. Finally, Belisarius was successful in defeating the Goths at their capital of Ravenna in A.D. 538, although they lingered on in the Italian peninsula and even retook considerable territory, until they were finally wiped out in A.D. 555. The turning point, however, had come when in A.D. 538 the city of Rome stood free of barbarian control for the first time in sixty years. The bishop of Rome assumed leadership of the city.

If it is agreed that two of the three horns uprooted by the little horn (vs. 8) were the Vandals (A.D. 534) and the Ostrogoths (A.D. 538/555), there is less agreement among historians about which was the third uprooted power. Some Adventist historians favor the Heruli, the tribe that conquered Rome in A.D. 476. The Heruli were later defeated by the Ostrogoths who were, in turn, defeated by the Roman general Belisarius. Thus the Heruli provide one possible identification for the third horn.

But the evidence seems to be in favor of the Visigoths as the third horn. For a time this tribe lived in southern France. There the Visigoths were eventually defeated by Clovis, king of the Franks, around A.D. 508. Although their power was largely destroyed at this time, the survivors were pushed into Spain where they were subjugated at last by a Moslem invasion in the eighth century A.D. Because the Visigoths were not eradicated by the Franks, some Bible historians have felt they should not be identified as the third horn uprooted before the little horn in Daniel's vision. It is not clear, however, that the prophecy requires total eradication to fulfill the symbol of being uprooted.

The three horns uprooted by the little horn can be identified, then, as the Vandals, the Ostrogoths, and the Visigoths (or the Heruli). All three had been in theological opposition to Rome over the nature of Christ's divinity. Their demise and thus the removal of their theological opposition made way for the even more widespread distribution of orthodox Roman Christianity. This might be seen as a welcome development for Christianity, but internal developments within the church had a negative impact upon the form of Christianity presented. The movement went awry, and thus the prophecy depicts this power as gathering religious power into its own hands in order to persecute those who did not recognize its authority (vss. 21, 25).

The four beast powers of chapter 7 all appear to be concerned with territorial expansion. The little horn, on the other hand, is clearly a religious power and is interested in distinctly religious issues. Bible students have long identified this little horn as the second phase of Rome, the first phase being the terrible beast of verse 7. What characteristics of this little horn does Daniel 7 give that would lead to such an interpretation?

Characteristics of the Little Horn

First, the little horn grows out of the fourth beast—among the ten horns. It comes out of the Roman beast (vss. 7, 8, 24), and therefore it must be in some way a continuation of the Roman Empire.

Second, the time of the little horn's appearance and the events which occurred at that time help to identify it. The ten horns of the Roman beast represent the divisions into which the Roman Empire fell. The little horn grew up among these ten horns, thus it grew up to its height of power *after* the barbarian tribes had divided the Roman Empire into pieces, that is, by the fifth or sixth centuries A.D. We have already seen how three horns, or powers, were uprooted by the power of the Roman emperor Justinian and the Franks, working together with the bishop of Rome.

A third characteristic of the little horn power is that it was to speak great or "boastful" words against the Most High God (vss. 8, 11, 20, 25). In addition to taking some of the titles previously carried by the Caesars, the bishop of Rome assumed religious titles and prerogatives that can be described only as "boastful" words.

What were some of these titles and functions assumed by the bishop of Rome?

He took the title, "Vicar of the Son of God," meaning that he stood in place of the Son of God to represent Him here on earth. Compare also the title of "holy father" with Jesus' comments about the use of that title in a religious setting (see Matthew 23:9). Note, too, the claim to be able to forgive sins through the rites of the confessional, whereas the Jews in Jesus' time considered His claim to forgive sins to be blasphemy (see Matthew 9:2-6).

The claim is made in a training manual for priests, *Dignities and Duties of the Priest;* or *Selva*, that God is obligated to come down upon the altar at the time of the mass, regardless of the spiritual state of the priest who officiates in that service! Thus man is not serving God, rather, God is under the control of man! (See pages 26, 27.) In a number of respects, the theological and titular claims of this religious power have exceeded those which are enjoined by Scripture.

A fourth characteristic is that the saints of the Most High were to be given into the power of the little horn and be oppressed by it. Thus the little horn would be a persecuting power (vs. 25). The Roman Church has upheld the principle of its right to persecute those who deny its religious authority. The *New Catholic Encyclopedia* states in its article on "Torture:"

Under the influence of Germanic customs and concepts, torture was little used from the 9th to the 12th centuries, but with the revival of Roman law the practice was reestablished in the 12th century. . . . In 1252 [Pope] Innocent IV sanctioned the infliction of torture by the civil authorities upon heretics, and torture came to have a recognized place in the procedure of the inquisitorial courts.

Writing from a strongly anti-Catholic position, the nineteenth-century historian W. E. H. Lecky wrote:

That the Church of Rome has shed more innocent blood than any other institution that has ever existed among mankind [up through the end of the nineteenth century], will be questioned by no Protestant who has a competent knowledge of history. The memorials, indeed, of many of her persecutions are now so scanty, that it is impossible to form a complete conception of the multitude of her victims, and it is quite certain that no powers of imagination can adequately realize their sufferings. Llorente, who had free access to the archives of the Spanish Inquisition, assures us that by that tribunal alone more than 31,000 persons were burnt, and more than 290,000 condemned to punishments less severe than death. The number of those who were put to death for their religion in the Netherlands alone, in the reign of Charles V., has been estimated by a very high authority at 50,000, and at least half as many perished under his son (Lecky, 2:40, 41).

At the other end of the scale are the writings of Robert Kingdom, who has attempted to downplay the effects of the St. Bartholomew's Day Massacre in France. In spite of his aim he admits:

The massacre did not stop with these killings. It spread to the general populace of Paris, as fanatical mobs killed hundreds, probably thousands, of Protestant residents of the city. The

THE ROMAN EMPIRE DIVIDED

Although boundaries were rather fluid, this map represents the general positions of the ten divisions of the Roman Empire as they were circa 476 A.D.

violence did not even stop in Paris; as news of what had occurred in the capital spread throughout the kingdom there were popular uprisings and massacres of Protestants in about a dozen other cities. Their aim was evidently to extirpate the entire Protestant movement, root and branch (Kingdom, 35).

As for the outcome of those massacres, Kingdom concludes:

> The massacres unleashed by the assassination of Coligny did not unify France religiously or even end violence between the religious communities. The royal government next turned to more concerted and calculated action, mobilizing royal armies to reduce the communities that remained under the control of defiant Protestants. That only moved the conflict to a different plane and created new types of martyrs for Goulart and other Protestant writers to memorialize. (Ibid., p. 50.)

One can also think of the crusades against the Waldenses of the Piedmont Valleys of northwestern Italy (see E. Comba, *History of the Waldenses of Italy*) and the Albigenses of southern France (see E. Ladurie, *Montaillou: The Promised Land of Terror*). This is a bloody record, but one which is sometimes excused by saying that the power of the state did this.

A fifth characteristic of the little horn power is that it would "try to change set times and the laws" (Daniel 7:25). The Aramaic word for "times" is *zimnin*, the plural form of *zeman*. When used in the singular, this word refers to a point in time, but as a plural, it refers to repeated points in time. These repeated points in time are connected in the very same Bible verse with God's law.

What law is this?

God has given various laws in the Old Testament, but the law of God *par excellence* is the law of the Ten Commandments (see Exodus 34:28; Deuteronomy 4:13; 10:4). The only provision regarding time in this most special law of God appears in the fourth commandment, which deals with the Sabbath, the seventh day (see Exodus 20:8-11). Earthly religious powers have endeavored to alter that commandment by transferring the obligation of the Sabbath to Sunday, even though there is no biblical command to do so. But the original divine precept remains unchanged, so these earthly powers only "think to change" (Daniel 7:25, KJV; "try to change," NIV) this law and its specification about time.

Not only have these earthly powers attempted to make this change, but they have also considered it to be a mark of their authority. The Roman Church says that it has received the *magesterium*, or teaching authority, from God and that this has enabled it to make this transfer.

Listen to John A. O'Brien, professor of theology at the University of Notre Dame from the 1940s to the 1960s on this point:

> The Bible does not contain all the teachings of the Christian religion, nor does it formulate all the duties of its members. Take, for example, the matter of Sunday observance, the attendance at divine services and the abstention from unnecessary servile work on that day, a matter upon which our Protestant neighbors have for many years laid great emphasis. Let me address myself in a friendly spirit to my dear nonCatholic reader:
>
> You believe that the Bible alone is a safe guide in religious matters. You also believe that one of the fundamental duties enjoined upon you by your Christian faith is that of Sunday observance. But where does the Bible speak of such an obligation? I have read the Bible from the first verse of Genesis to the last verse of Revelations [sic], and have found no reference to the duty of sanctifying the Sunday. The day mentioned in the Bible is not the Sunday, the first day of the week but the Saturday, the last day of the week.
>
> It was the Apostolic Church which, acting by virtue of that authority conferred upon her by Christ, changed the observance to the Sunday in honor of the day on which Christ rose from the dead, and to signify that now we are no longer under the Old Law of the Jews, but under the New Law of Christ. In observing the Sunday as you do, is it not apparent that you are really acknowledging the insufficiency of the Bible

alone as a rule of faith and religious conduct, and proclaiming the need of a divinely established teaching authority which in theory you deny? (O'Brien, 138,139).

A bit further in his treatment, O'Brien reinforces that argument and makes it even more explicit:

> The third [fourth in the thinking of most Protestants] commandment is: "Remember thou keep holy the Sabbath Day." Like the first two commandments, this one also concerns our duties to God, Particularly the duty to worship Him on a designated day. The word "Sabbath" means rest, and is Saturday the seventh day of the week.
>
> Why then do Christians observe Sunday instead of the day mentioned in the Bible? . . .
>
> The Church received the authority to make such a change from her Founder, Jesus Christ. He solemnly conferred upon His Church the power to legislate, govern and administer . . . the power of the keys. It is to be noted that the Church did not change the divine law obliging men to worship, but merely changed the day on which such public worship was to be offered; thus the law involved was merely a ceremonial law.
>
> But since Saturday, not Sunday, is specified in the Bible, isn't it curious that non-Catholics who profess to take their religion directly from the Bible and not from the Church, observe Sunday instead of Saturday? Yes, of course, it is inconsistent; but this change was made about fifteen centuries before Protestantism was born, and by that time the custom was universally observed. They have continued the custom, even though it rests upon the authority of the Catholic Church and not upon an explicit text in the Bible. That observance remains as a reminder of the Mother Church from which the non-Catholic sects broke away—like a boy running away from home but still carrying in his pocket a picture of his mother or a lock of her hair (O'Brien, 406-408).

These claims stand in opposition to the plain and simple truth of the Word of God that "the seventh day is the Sabbath of the Lord thy God" (Exodus 20:10, KJV).

Daniel 7:25 says that the religious power identified by the various characteristics of the little horn would make an attempt to change a particular type of time, a repeated point in time that is connected with God's law. This prediction fits precisely with the role of the little horn in regard to God's seventh-day Sabbath. Thus this characteristic of the little horn can be added to those other characteristics listed above.

The final characteristic of the little horn found in the prophecy is noted in Daniel 7:25: "The saints will be handed over to him for a time, times, and half a time." What is a "time"?

In Daniel 4, as we have seen, a "time" refers to a year. Seven "times" were to pass over Nebuchadnezzar until he regained his sanity (4:16, 23, 25, 32). The "time, times, and half a time" of Daniel 7:25, then, equal three and a half prophetic years. Each year is made up of 360 days, making a total of 1,260 days. The year-for-a-day principle gives us 1,260 actual years (see Ezekiel 4:6; Numbers 14:34). A fuller discussion of the year-for-a-day principle is found in chapters 6 and 7 of volume 2 of this study on Daniel. Revelation 12:6, 14 confirms this calculation. There, verse 6 refers to 1,260 days which are equivalent to "a time, times, and half a time" in verse 14.

The question then becomes: Where in the course of the history of the little horn, or papacy, should we place these 1,260 years? To what period do they best correspond?

As noted above, the transition from Imperial Rome to medieval Rome took place in the sixth century A.D. With that transition, Imperial Rome faded away, and the papacy came to the forefront, occupying the position of leadership in Rome vacated by the political power. The particular point at which the papal power began to be realized was when the Ostrogoths' control of Rome was lifted in A.D. 538. Prior to that time, the bishop of Rome had been under the control of barbarian tribes for more than sixty years. Now, free of that encumbrance, his authority, both civil and religious, began to increase until the medieval papacy reached its zenith in the eleventh through the thirteenth centuries.

In A.D. 533, the events of A.D. 538 had been foreshadowed by a decree which Emperor Justinian issued from Constantinople proclaiming the bishop of Rome head of all the churches. This decree arose out of certain theological controversies and resulted in the emperor confirming to Pope John II the headship of all the churches. All the correspondence relating to this decree was codified as *Corpus Iuris Civilis* (book 1, title 1, 7). It was reconfirmed by Justinian's *Novella* 9 in A.D. 535 and again in *Novella* 131 in A.D. 545. (A text of all three of these decrees can be found in L. E. Froom, *Prophetic Faith of Our Fathers*, vol. 1.)

In A.D. 538, thanks to the emperor's troops, the Roman bishop was in a position to assume the headship of the church in fact and not just on paper. Another decree by Justinian given in 555, the year of the final defeat of the Ostrogoths, cemented both the religious and political authority of the papacy. Since the military liberation of the papacy was a central event in this series of events, without which the other decrees would never have become effective, it is appropriate to date the "time, times, and half a time" (Dan. 7:25) of papal authority as beginning in A.D. 538.

The endpoint is even more sharply defined. It came on February 15, 1798, when the French general, Berthier, deposed Pope Pius VI and exiled him to France, where he died in July 1799. Not until 1801, when Napoleon signed a concordat with Pius VII, did the first stirrings of a revived papacy take place. For a time it appeared as if the papacy had received a "deadly wound" in 1798, but from that nadir in its experience it has gradually arisen to a new state of prominence in the world (see Revelation 13:3).

Summary

The characteristics of the little horn as given in the prophecy of Daniel 7 may be summarized as follows.

First, the little horn comes out of the Roman beast; therefore, it is Roman in character. Second, it comes up after the divisions of Rome, represented by the ten horns, had taken place. Third, three of those horns were to be plucked up before it. Fourth, growing from smallness, this power came to speak boasting words against the Most High, fulfilled in the presumptuous claims of this religious power. Fifth, it was also to be a persecuting power, as amply attested by the various crusades and inquisitions that it has conducted. Sixth, it would also make an attack upon God's law, especially that part which has to do with a repeated point in time such as the Sabbath.

Regarding this last point, the church claims the change of the Sabbath to Sunday to be a mark of its authority. The 1957 edition of Peter Geiermann's *Convert's Catechism of Catholic Doctrine* makes this claim:

> Q. *Which is the Sabbath day?*
> A. Saturday is the Sabbath day.
> Q. *Why do we observe Sunday instead of Saturday?*
> A. We observe Sunday instead of Saturday because the Catholic Church transferred the solemnity from Saturday to Sunday (50).

Geiermann's catechism simply reiterates a claim made at the Council of Trent in the late sixteenth century A.D. in response to the charges of the Protestant Reformation. The Council decreed: "The Church of God has thought it well to transfer the celebration and observance of the Sabbath to Sunday" (McHugh and Callan, 402).

The Catholic historian V. J. Kelly has also made this point:

> Some theologians have held that God likewise directly determined the Sunday as the day of worship in the New Law, that He Himself has explicitly substituted the Sunday for the Sabbath. But this theory is now entirely abandoned. It is now commonly held that God simply gave His Church the power to set aside whatever day, or days, she would deem suitable as Holy Days. The Church chose Sunday; the first day of the week, and in the course of time added other days, as holy days. (Kelly, 2).

He continues:

> The fact, however, that Christ until His death, and His Apostles at least for a time after Christ's Ascension, observed the Sabbath is evidence enough that our Lord Himself did not substitute the Lord's day for the Sabbath, during His lifetime on earth. Instead, as most agree, He simply gave His Church the power to determine the days to be set aside for the special worship of God. . . . It is easy to surmise that this preference of Christ for the first day of the week greatly influenced the Apostles and the early Christians to keep that day holy, and eventually moved them to make a complete substitution of the Sabbath for the Sunday. There is no conclusive evidence, however, that the Apostles made this change of days by a definite decree (ibid.).

As a final characteristic of the little horn power, the prophecy allots it a certain period of time—three and a half "times"—for the exercise of its authority. This symbolic time period, interpreted according to the year-for-a-day principle, extended from A. D. 538, when Rome and its bishop were liberated from the stranglehold of the Ostrogoths, to A. D. 1798 when the pope was taken prisoner and exiled from Rome, thus temporarily ending his dominion and authority.

Thus, all seven of the characteristics given in the prophecy fit the Roman Church and no other power, identifying it firmly with the symbol of the little horn. By way of caution, we must be careful to maintain a distinction between a theological system and the administrative center of a church, on the one hand, and the conscience of the individual Christian, on the other. Only God knows the motives of an individual, and He alone can read the human heart. As the great judge, He will determine each person's sincerity and devotion in His great final judgment. The focus in Daniel's prophecy is not on individual Christians, but on a religious system that has gone awry—a system that has adopted unbiblical theological principles rooted in Greek philosophy. It is this system that the prophecy identifies and from which it calls for separation (see Revelation 18:1-4). An individual Christian can still act in good conscience within that communion, but once light becomes known, it is time for him or her to act accordingly.

The prophecy of Daniel 7 does not end with the career of any of the four beasts that it portrays. Nor does it conclude with the actions of the little horn. Dark though the picture is, God has an answer to all this sinful human history. It is God's answer; it is not of human devising. God's answer lies in the process whereby He leads His people into His kingdom—the divine judgment, the coming of the Son of Man, and the vindication of God's saints. These topics, as described in the prophecy of chapter 7, fit best with the prophetic themes to be discussed in the second volume of this study on Daniel and will be treated fully there.

The Results

We need to keep in mind that this prophecy was written by Daniel in the sixth century B.C. at the time God gave it to him. With the exception of Babylon, none of the world kingdoms brought to view were yet on the stage of world history as the superpowers they would become. Yet the history subsequent to Daniel's time has fulfilled the prophecy precisely. There have been four, and only four, world powers that arose on the scene of action—not two or three or five or seven, but four. Each of these four powers can be identified, and it can be demonstrated that they did indeed manifest the characteristics depicted in the symbolic prophecy. The prophecy predicts with precision the onward march of Babylon, Medo-Persia, Greece, and Rome. Looking back through the centuries from our vantage point in history, we can trace the fulfillment of Daniel's prophecy and see how the specifications are matched evenly by the procession of kingdoms that arose and fell in the Mediterranean region. Following the succession of these four kingdoms, the little horn, representing the medieval papacy that arose out of the ruins of Imperial Rome, appeared as foretold. It, too, acted out the activities predicted in the prophecy until the end of the time allotted to it. Shortly after that time, according to the prophecy, God was to take up His work of judgment in response to this procession of human powers (see 7:22,

26). The reality of the judgment and the establishment of God's everlasting kingdom is just as certain as has been the fulfillment of the earlier stages of the historic panorama of Daniel 7. The procession of human powers expressed by the beasts and the horns sets the stage for God's final and decisive action in history.

One way to study the Bible and understand it better is to look for key words—words that appear over and over in a biblical narrative. In Daniel 7, such a key word is repeated and repeated—the Aramaic word translated "dominion." This word occurs seven times in chapter 7 (vss. 6, 12, 14 , 26, 27). The NIV translates this word more broadly as "authority" (vss. 6, 12), "dominion" (vs. 14), "power" (vss. 26, 27), and "rulers" (vs. 27). This variety of translational equivalents weakens the impact of the repetition of this key word. When we realize that the word "dominion" is repeated over and over again in this chapter, it becomes evident that it provides a key to understanding this chapter.

In terms of ordinary human political entities, dominion, or authority, appears to be rather transitory. Babylon had it for a while, but then it lost it to Persia. Persia had it for a little longer time, but still lost it to Greece. Strong as Greece first appeared under Alexander the Great, it soon lost dominion too. Rome, which looked like an eternal kingdom, did not last nearly as long as expected, and it, too, lost its dominion. At the noontide of the papacy in the twelfth century, it looked as though it might maintain an eternal dominion, but it, too, came to a loss of dominion.

Is this all that human beings have to look forward to? Is the eternal fate of humanity to be subject to this constant change in the cycle of earthly rulers, most of whom are self-serving and oppressive?

God's answer is No! There will come a time when He will set up His kingdom, and His kingdom is going to be different from any that humanity has seen previously (vs. 27). Not only will it be different in character, being based upon love and justice and grace, but it will also be different in terms of time. It will not be temporary and transitory like all the earthly entities that have gone before it. This kingdom will be eternal; its dominion will go on forever. Thus there is a contrast in the way the word *dominion* is used in this chapter.

When it is used of earthly human governments, it refers to something temporary and transitory. But when it is used of God's government, it is eternal. The dominion of God and His kingdom will last forever and ever. That is one of the precious promises of this prophecy. And that kingdom will soon come, for we have almost reached the end of the line of history depicted in the prophecy of this chapter.

Daniel 7 marks a transition point in Daniel's book. It marks the transition from the mostly historical first half of the book to the fully prophetic section in the second half. That is why chapter 7 contains both history and prophecy—although more prophecy than history. It foreshadows the prophetic last half of Daniel's book. The transition to apocalyptic prophecy begins in this chapter without waiting for the second section of the book.

But chapter 7 also has ties to the historical half of Daniel. It is anchored in that section by its language, being the last chapter written in Aramaic. It is anchored there by its location in the book, integrated into the literary structure of that portion of the book.

Now that the study of all of the historical section of Daniel's book is complete, it is appropriate to again review the chiastic outline of that section as a whole:

A. Daniel 2—Fallen kingdoms (the great image)
   B. Daniel 3—Kingly persecution (the fiery furnace)
      C. Daniel 4—Fallen king (Nebuchadnezzar's madness)
      C. Daniel 5—Fallen king (Belshazzar's last night)
   B. Daniel 6—Kingly persecution (the lions' den)
A. Daniel 7—Fallen kingdoms (beasts rise and fall)

In this outline, we can see visually that similar content ties together chapters 4 and 5, chapters 3 and 6, and chapters 2 and 7. That is why we have discussed them in this order. Thus the literary structure has a bearing on our interpretation and shows that Daniel 7 is indeed a further and more detailed explanation of what has already gone on before in more simple terms in Daniel 2. Daniel 2 and 7 are complementary in content and complementary in literary structural location.

At this point, our study of the first half of Daniel is complete, with the exception of the conclusion of chapter 7 that has been reserved for the second volume of this study.

■ Applying the Word

Daniel 2, 7

1. In practical terms, does it mean anything to my faith that God can predict the course of history and the rise and fall of nations? If so, how does this affect my faith?
2. What do these chapters tell me about the certainty of the second coming of Jesus? How *should* that knowledge affect my daily life? How *does* it do so? In what ways can the gap be closed between how it *should* and how it *does* affect my life? What can I do about the situation today?
3. Does the history presented in these chapters appear to me as a reality or as an abstraction? In what ways is my life a part of the plan of this history?
4. In what ways does chapter 7 highlight the issues in the great controversy between God and Satan? What are some of the issues in that controversy as revealed in chapter 7? How is my daily life placing me on one side or the other of these issues? In what ways do I need to change in order to be on God's side? How can I do so? What steps can I take?

■ Researching the Word

1. Compare the beast from the sea in Revelation 13 with Daniel 7. List all the symbolic connections between the two chapters that you can discover. To which of the symbols in Daniel 7 does the sea beast of Revelation 13 correspond? Compare the two in parallel columns. What information regarding the sea beast helps us fill out our understanding of the cor-

responding power in Daniel 7?

2. With the help of a concordance, look up all biblical references in Daniel and Revelation to 1,260 days; time, times, and half a time; and forty-two months. In context, how do these texts add to your understanding of the symbol in Daniel 7? What information do they add?

3. Compare the characteristics of the little horn as given in Daniel 7 with those given in chapter 8. Are both chapters referring to the same power? In your Daniel notebook, list the evidence for your conclusions.

4. Follow Daniel's personal prophetic experience through chapter 7. When does he see the vision, and where does the vision stop? When does he talk with the interpreting angel, and when does the interpreting angel talk to him? How many times does this discussion go back and forth between them? What do you learn from this about how prophets received information from God and how the prophetic gift operated?

■ Further Study of the Word

1. To research the history behind the rise and fall of the kingdoms of Babylon, Medo-Persia, Greece, and Rome, check with the appropriate sections of the *Encyclopedia Britannica*, the *Encyclopedia Americana*, or the *Cambridge Ancient History*.

2. For a special study on the break-up of Alexander the Great's empire, see F. D. Nichol, ed., *The SDA Bible Commentary*, 4:823-826.

3. For further background on the interpretation of the 1,260 prophetic days—Daniel's three and a half times—see the massive documentation found in L. E. Froom, the *Prophetic Faith of Our Fathers*. See especially the last sections of volume 2.

4. For a more detailed view of the interpretation of Daniel 7 than that which has been presented here, consult C. Mervyn Maxwell, *God Cares*, 1:109-143.